HOPE IS LONELY

KIM SEUNG-HEE
HOPE IS LONELY

Translated by
Brother Anthony of Taizé

Introduced by
John Kinsella

Published by Arc Publications,
Nanholme Mill, Shaw Wood Road
Todmorden OL14 6DA, UK
www.arcpublications.co.uk

Copyright: © Kim Seung-Hee, 2021
Translation copyright © Brother Anthony of Taizé, 2021
Translator's Preface copyright © Brother Anthony of Taizé, 2021
Introduction copyright © John Kinsella, 2021
Copyright in the present edition © Arc Publications, 2021

978 1911469 76 6 (pbk)

ACKNOWLEDGEMENTS
Poems from *Hope is Lonely* and *A Croaker on a Chopping Board*
by Kim Seung-Hee were originally published by
the Munhakdongne Publishing Corporation / Nanda (Korea),
and are reproduced here with their permission.

Design by Tony Ward

Cover photograph:
'Feathers' by Tony Ward

This book is in copyright. Subject to statutory exception and
to provision of relevant collective licensing agreements, no
reproduction of any part of this book may take place without
the written permission of Arc Publications.

This book is translated and published with the support of the
Literature Translation Institute of Korea (LTI Korea)

Arc Publications 'Visible Poets' series
Series Editor: Jean Boase-Beier

CONTENTS

Series Editor's Note / 7
Translator's Preface / 9
Introduction / 15

from
HOPE IS LONELY

24 / 희망에는 신의 물방울이 들어있다 •	Inside of Hope is God's Water Drop / 25
24 / 반투명한 불투명 •	Translucent Opacity / 25
26 / 희망의 연옥 •	Hope's Purgatory / 27
26 / 그래도라는 섬이 있다 •	There's an Island Called "Nevertheless" / 27
30 / 하얀 접시에 올라온 하얀 가자미 한 마리 •	One White Flatfish Lying on a White Dish / 31
32 / 말은 울고 있다 •	A Word is Weeping / 33
34 / 자유인의 꿈 •	Dream of Someone Free / 35
34 / 매화는 힘이 세다 •	Plum Blossom is Mighty / 35
36 / 바람을 옷에 싼 여자 •	Woman Wrapping the Wind in Clothes / 37
38 / 여자가 낳은 것 •	What Women Give Birth to / 39
40 / 시의 응급실에서 •	In Poetry's Emergency Room / 41
40 / 모래 거울 •	Sand Mirror / 41
44 / 낙원 역 •	Paradise Stop / 45
46 / 전위의 사람 •	Avant-gardists / 47
48 / 달걀 속의 생 6 •	Life in the Egg 6 / 49
52 / 달걀 속의 생 7 •	Life in the Egg 7 / 53
56 / 달걀 속의 생 8 •	Life in the Egg 8 / 57
58 / 천의 아리랑 •	A Thousand *Arirangs* / 59
58 / 1. 가슴 속의 피아노 •	1. Piano in the Breast / 59
60 / 2. 부용산 •	2. Buyong Mountain / 61
62 / 3. 론도 카프리치오소 •	3. Rondo Capriccioso / 63
64 / 4. 배고픈 승냥이의 노래 •	4. *The Song of a Hungry Coyote* / 65
64 / 5. 밥의 아리랑 •	5. *Rice Arirang* / 65
66 / 6. 흙 보다 아름다운 책은 없다 •	6. *There Is No Book More Lovely than Clay* / 67
70 / 희망이 외롭다 •	Hope Is Lonely / 71
72 / 서울의 우울 6 •	Seoul Melancholy 6 / 73
74 / 서울의 우울 7 •	Seoul Melancholy 7 / 75
76 / 서울의 우울 8 •	Seoul Melancholy 8 / 77
78 / 서울의 우울 9 •	Seoul Melancholy 9 / 79
78 / 서울의 우울 10	Seoul Melancholy 10 / 79

from
A CROAKER ON A CHOPPING BOARD

84 / 꽃들의 제사 • Flowers' Memorial Rites / 85
84 / 맨드라미의 시간에 • Cockscomb Time / 85
86 / 오른편 심장 하나 주세요 • Give me a Heart on the Right-Hand Side / 8
88 / 해바라기와 꿀벌 • Sunflower and Honeybee / 89
88 / 칼갈이 광고 차 • The Knife Grinder's Advertising Car / 89
90 / 작년의 달력 • Last Year's Calendar / 91
92 / 한겨울 밤의 서정시 • A Midwinter Night's Lyric Poem / 93
94 / 전망 • Prospect / 95
96 / 좌파/우파/허파 • Left / Right / Lungs / 97
98 / '알로하'라는 말 • The Word 'Aloha' / 99
98 / 노숙의 일가친척 • One Family Sleeping Out / 99
100 / 우체국과 헌 구두 • The Post Office and Old Shoes / 101
102 / '이미'라는 말 2 • The Word 'Already' 2 / 103
104 / 알로하 꽃목걸이 • Aloha, Leis of Welcome / 105
104 / 여행으로의 초대 • Invitation to a Journey / 105
106 / 트로이의 시간 • Troy Time / 107
108 / 푸른 점화 • Blue Ignition / 109
110 / 꽃피는 아몬드 나무 • An Almond Tree in Bloom / 111
112 / 내 속에 내가 마트료시카 • Inside, I'm a Matryoshka Doll / 113
114 / 멍게 • Sea Squirt / 115
114 / 아무도 아무것도 • Nobody and Nothing / 115
116 / 막막한 시간 • Boundless Time / 117
118 / 애도 시계 • Mourning's Clock / 119
118 / 저녁의 잔치 • Evening's Party / 119
122 / 가족사진 • Family Photos / 123
124 / 거대한 팽이 • A Huge Top / 125
126 / 목에 걸린 뼈 • A Bone Caught in the Throat / 127

Biographical Notes / 129

SERIES EDITOR'S NOTE

The 'Visible Poets' series was established in 2000, and set out to challenge the view that translated poetry could or should be read without regard to the process of translation it had undergone. Since then, things have moved on. Today there is more translated poetry available and more debate on its nature, its status, and its relation to its original. We know that translated poetry is neither English poetry that has mysteriously arisen from a hidden foreign source, nor is it foreign poetry that has silently rewritten itself in English. We are more aware that translation lies at the heart of all our cultural exchange; without it, we must remain artistically and intellectually insular.

One of the aims of the series was, and still is, to enrich our poetry with the very best work that has appeared elsewhere in the world. And the poetry-reading public is now more aware than it was at the start of this century that translation cannot simply be done by anyone with two languages. The translation of poetry is a creative act, and translated poetry stands or falls on the strength of the poet-translator's art. For this reason 'Visible Poets' publishes only the work of the best translators, and gives each of them space, in a Preface, to talk about the trials and pleasures of their work.

From the start, 'Visible Poets' books have been bilingual. Many readers will not speak the languages of the original poetry but they, too, are invited to compare the look and shape of the English poems with the originals. Those who can are encouraged to read both. Translation and original are presented side-by-side because translations do not displace the originals; they shed new light on them and are in turn themselves illuminated by the presence of their source poems. By drawing the readers' attention to the act of translation itself, it is the aim of these books to make the work of both the original poets and their translators more visible.

Jean Boase-Beier

TRANSLATOR'S PREFACE

For many years now, Kim Seung-Hee and I have been colleagues and good friends, starting in the days when we were both teaching at Sogang University in Seoul, I in the English Department and she in the Korean Department. She had completed her undergraduate studies in that same university, majoring in English, before going on to pursue graduate studies in the Korean Department. My office was on the ground floor and hers on the floor above, so we would often bump into each other on the stairs, each hurrying toward a classroom, her arms always more heavily loaded with books than mine were. Now we are both retired and we remain close. In February 2017, we went with two other Korean poets to Hawaii University, UC Berkeley, and Stanford University to introduce Korean literature and read poetry together.

She has published ten poetry collections, including *Concerto for the Left Hand* (1983), *Life in the Egg* (1989), *Pots Bobbing* (2006), *Hope is Lonely* (2012), and *Croaker on a Chopping Board* (2017), as well as four volumes of academic prose, including, *Studies in the Poetry of Yi Sang* (1998), *The Semiotic Chora and Korean Poetry* (2008), *Modern Poetry of Mourning and Depression* (2015), and two novels, including *On the Road to Santa Fe* (1997). Her most widely-read books are her autobiographical essays, *Pensées on Turning 33* (1985), and an annotated anthology of Korean women poets, *Men Have No Idea* (2001). Both books were highly popular at the time of publication and are still widely read today. Two volumes of translated poems have been published in the United States: *I Want to Hijack an Airplane* (Homa & Sekey, 2004) and *Walking on a Washing Line* (Cornell University, 2011). One critic has written, very acutely "I find her poems very heavy, very oppressive and depressing as a whole. They capture our painful history, our lives as women, our ontological anguish, and our painful stories with a keen eye. They are not poems that you can read comfortably, they don't make you feel happy, but they have the power to make you squirm." But that is not the whole story.

In the early 1970s, Kim Seung-Hee began her career as a poet when the poem 'Water in a Picture' won the *Gyeonghyang Newspaper*'s Spring New Writer's Award. This initial recognition is standard practice in Korea. At the time, she was regarded as a highly unusual poet, a female modernist and stylist, and therefore did not always receive favourable reviews from male critics. That was because nationalistic and populist literature were then the dominant influences in Korea.

She was also deeply interested in Greek mythology, influenced by her husband, who studied Greek philosophy. In one of her first poems, 'Sun Mass,' she sang the desires of the harsh gods and the tragic condition of human beings in surreal language. However, after the birth of her children in the 1980s, she began to discover her body and voice as a woman, and from then on she began to focus on male-centred realities.

The 1980s was a time when the democratization movement was very strong in Korea, and one result of that was the way the voices of women, workers and the weak began to be foregrounded. During the 1980s, she became more strongly aware of her identity as a woman, started using strongly female, feminist voices in her poems, especially in her second collection, *Concerto for the Left Hand* (1983). She calls that "the transformation from being my father's daughter to being my mother's daughter." At the time, Korea was still a very traditional patriarchal society, and she had come to feel that she was one with her mother's body, that like her mother she possessed the voice of "one excluded," and like her was a woman walking in the dark. She wrote a sequence of five poems, 'Love Song for the Belly-Button', and two of them are now considered significant enough to be included in middle and high school literature textbooks.

(...)
We are equal in our belly-buttons.
They are the scars of our birthdays, the name-tags of orphans,
the gentle grass of our flesh,
the vermilion lips of the white skeleton painted with phosphate bite first.
We are so equal in our belly-buttons.

Dear You, whoever you are, if you have not abandoned your belly-button, I heartily forgive you. When I see, in the springtime, new shoots budding on barren branches, when I see birds spring suddenly into the air, I feel my belly-button itching as if with eczema. And now my belly-button is not in the past-perfect tense, but it is budding, as always, in the present-progressive of my life. And Mother... ah, Mother... as I say this, I recall a woman walking along the beach, weeping. Pursuing her sorrow, her love, and her despair, my belly-button enters the womb at the beginning of time. Mother!... Mother! My secret entry into compassion and damnation... Our dear Mother...!

'Love Song for the Belly-Button, 1'
translated by Kay Richards & Steffen F. Richards

In one of her essays, she has written about the belly-button metaphor:

> The belly-button is the point where my mother's umbilical cord was joined to me. The belly-button is a scrap of my mother's flesh buried in mine, a sign of being an orphan, the symbol of the "abandonment" that existentialist philosophy talks about. The belly-button is also a portable mother that we always carry about with us. When I am having a hard time, undergoing trials, I sometimes sense my mother's voice ringing in my belly-button, telling me to bear up. It may be a form of narcissism, but I tend to think that human beings need a kindly second-person world nearby, in order to go on living. Because of the belly-button, we can never completely leave our mother behind, and through it we always receive her compassionate protection. The navel is a sign of the origin of life created by the women of the world and the sign of being an abandoned orphan.

There are probably very few poets in the world who have written so many poems about their navel.

In 1985, when she was 33 years old, she wrote a set of autobiographical essays titled *Pensées on Turning 33*, which was very popular, being read by many and selling well. She said she had wanted to write a book like James Joyce's autobiographical *A Portrait of the Artist as a Young Man* or Sylvia Plath's biographical novel *Bell Jar*. Anyway, the book earned her from one critic the nicknames "Lover of Fire", "Terrorist of Language" and "Shaman of Surrealism". Like American confessional poets such as Robert Lowell, Sylvia Plath and Ann Sexton, she freely confessed everything, stories about her family, feuds with her younger brother whom her mother adored, the dangerous agonies of her adolescence, curiosity about suicide, anxious feelings of love, the covert wounds resulting from mental crises arising from being a woman, psychological crises, all mingled with vivid fictions. The boldness and freedom of those confessions aroused readers' intense sympathy.

She wrote many poems about the trivial things that form part of a woman's everyday life – eggs in the refrigerator, pots, brooms, washing lines or chopping boards, attempting to expand them into problems related to universal human existence. Her main poetic orientation is a world of the imagination, intent as she is on evoking universal destinies through trivial everyday life and ordinary objects.

She has written

> Poetry is a world of the imagination that begins with the loneliness and pain of a first-person persona but does not neglect social pain, but rather accompanies it. Thanks to the poem, the first-person can go beyond the first-person and "I" can become "we." The eggs, pots, brooms, washing lines, flounders, croakers, and cutting boards that I evoke in my poems are metaphors of fragile and endangered women's existence, as well as being universal human metaphors. I desperately go rowing across a first-person world in an attempt to reach a universal sea.

Her husband majored in Greek philosophy and Plato and was for more than twenty years a university professor of philosophy. He was a very sincere and open-hearted man. Then suddenly, still young, he suffered a stroke while he was teaching a class. He struggled on for over a decade, before finally passing away in September 2014. She experienced intense fear and anguish, with the discovery of the futility and vulnerability of human existence. They had two children. Their daughter is now a professor in New York while their son works as an accountant in Toronto.

The present volume of English translations of Kim Seung-Hee's most recent poems is drawn half from her ninth collection, *Hope is Lonely*, and half from her tenth collection, *Croaker on a Chopping Board*. These two collections focus in multiple ways on humanity's utter fragility, through the themes of futility, death, despair, hope and mourning. Depression and love are also major themes. In her most recent volumes, her poems have come closer to the roots of human sorrow, while growing gentler in tone and imagery, and the collections include more poems about death, God, hope, and love.

First of all, these two collections contain numerous lyrics of sorrowful womanhood. Among the poignantly beautiful poems are 'Woman Wrapping the Wind in Clothes' and 'What Women Give Birth To'. These are songs of grief sung by a woman facing up to the winds of futility. Second, there are poems expressive of the grief arising from death. How is the death of a loved one to be interpreted? For it is only by interpreting death that we can mourn the dead properly. How can we transcend the fear of death? Since Nature and human life are so closely linked, hers is a somewhat romantic vision of death, in which no death ever occurs outside of the vast Chain of Being. In the poem

'One White Flatfish Lying on a White Dish', life and death are seen in a modernistic mode, whereas she adopts a romantic attitude when she sings about death seen in isolation. She sometimes sounds modernist and sometimes romantic. The roots of such contradictions lie deep within her. In the poem 'Flowers' Memorial Rites' she seeks salvation for the loneliness and isolation of a solitary individual who is bound to die by turning to the power of infinite Nature:

> What yearning can be making that sea of dahlia-like flowers bloom red?
> What yearning can be making that blue wave weep in my veins?
> What yearning is pushing that cloud?
> What yearning can be making the sunlight flutter as it sparkles on that flowing stream?
> What yearning links severed fingernail with severed fingernail?
> What yearning can be making that pebble forget gravity and float?
> What yearning enables a cicada to spend 17 years underground?
> What yearning brings together that vapour trail and this vapour trail?
> The heart now looking at that blue sky is racing.
> A blazing heart is the flowers' memorial rites.
> Now hot steam like that from a sulphuric hot spring
> is billowing up in this heart of mine.

Third, while composing numerous poems about women's issues, she has also written poems expressing a sharply critical consciousness regarding civilization in general, political and social issues, as well as entertaining poems that lightly psychoanalyse Korean society and culture. 'Left / Right / Lungs' is one such poem. She has written many poems that criticize, psychoanalyse, and mock Korean culture, but underneath them all is an immense sense of melancholy. Depression is a major topic in her poems, one expressed at length in the series of poems titled 'Seoul Melancholy.'

Fourth, she has written many language poems focusing on the Korean language itself. She frequently uses word-play, or undertakes various linguistic experiments such as homonyms and repetition of consonants, and has made radical experiments with using familiar Korean adverbial phrases as images or poetic contexts. It seems that her mother tongue is the very foundation of her existence as a poet, that she loves the Korean language with a deep affection. Given the immense gap separating Korean from the way the English language works, these language poems are hardly accessible for those who do not know Korean perfectly, and are almost impossible to translate convincingly, so that very few are included in the present selection.

Kim Seung-Hee seems to think that although humans are eager for freedom, they can never be free from the prisons of time and body, that the only ways leading to freedom are God's eternity and death. Was she influenced by Schopenhauer? She often says, "The self has to die before there is freedom," and has a special fondness for the arts, such as painting and music, which serve as a pathway into the Eternal. In order to gain distance from her own self, she enjoys travelling to far-off places, not only the United States and Canada, but also to exotic places such as Venice or Cairo, as can be seen in the poem 'Invitation to a Journey'. From the beginning, she seems to have had a deep belief in art as healing. For her, poetry is an absolute therapy, a means of healing by which she treats her pain and despair.

At times she enjoys writing poems that sound dark, even frightening, yet she herself is not dark, rather she insists that she is light-hearted, enjoys jokes, wit and paradoxes, laughing even in the very midst of hardships and trials. She says that, like a tree, she has a heliotropism and loves the sun, so that she instinctively turns toward what is bright, that she likes to walk slowly in the sunshine, welcoming it on her body as if recharging her solar batteries. It is to be hoped that those reading her poems in translation will feel a similar warming, invigorating effect.

Brother Anthony of Taizé

INTRODUCTION

"Hope does not grow straight…"
                    ('Inside of Hope is God's Water Drop')

Kim Seung-Hee's poetry sees traditional Korean forms responding to European, and later American, modernism by opening up to create liberated space, with the tensions between the external image and the interior processing of experience, between the subject and the object, between the idea and its manifestation in our lives, creating a complex and interactive poetics. From the city to the country, from the rural to the industrial, from the meditative to the violent realities of history and contemporary existence, poem after poem confronts and wrestles with what's encountered.

Here is a poet who is constantly struggling with thoughts and fears of death, of self-annihilation, and yet we know hope is close, no matter how despairing a poem becomes. One of my favourite images in this book is from the otherwise grim 'Seoul Melancholy 9':

birds that penetrate people's sorrows,
each being a bird
with a beautiful soul
                    ('Seoul Melancholy 9' p. 79)

The poet's distress is for the body and soul of the city as well as for the self fragmenting under stress, and through this, the poet of such introversion becomes a bardic speaker for her community. As we move back and forth through Kim Seung-Hee's poetry, we realise that if hope is there – and it *is* there, in the sun, the body, the shared experience of women, in art and in nature – it is not easy to conjure and not easy to sustain, though sustain it we must, in order to rectify the wrongs.

Kim Seung-Hee seems to me to be a poet of concrete possibilities set against mutable conversations. As Brother Anthony notes, she is a follower of the sun, despite darkness and dread being necessary accompaniments to its glory. This does not mean she is fatalistic, but intensely engaged with the far frontiers of life and death, and if, as the critics note, there is a prevailing sadness, I would argue that it is a necessary constant to make poetry speak out.

In her explorations of the voice of women in contemporary Korean society against the background of Korean history, we encounter writing about the body that reflects its impact on the world *outside the body*. So when Brother Anthony notes the "centrality" of the "navel" image of connection to the mother, the "I"-"we" relationship (that necessarily flows both ways), and the father's daughter becoming the mother's daughter, we might add the changing ways of seeing the reconfiguring of the relationship between a body in servitude and the objects that body is "forced" to use in domestic life. The cutting board, the plate with the dead fish that is to be carved up, the processes of giving and taking (in terms of gender, a "done deal" in conservative patriarchal society) segue with the aspirations of art to transcend, to locate, to temporise and to represent.

If this sounds like a confluence of "East" and "West" sensibilities, in many ways, given the poet's interest in Greek philosophy and myth, it is not surprising. If "woman" is aligned with the elemental, she is also part of her community, and ultimately herself – relationships which are anchored in the "ordinary" reality of everyday objects, tasks and acts, but are in a state of flux. In the poem 'Woman Wrapping the Wind in Clothes' the wind is as elemental as it gets: as artistic construct, it is a variable that the poet as woman can invert, since: "generation after generation, she robes the wind in clothes". The singular is collective, and across time the selves connect and work to give structure to "freedom", the irony being that the wind is a response, rather than a liberty or a choice – it acts as the air pressure directs. With the poem 'Plum Blossom is Mighty' we get to the point of reference we depart from as humans, but in 'Sand Mirror' we are returned to a world of illusions and we ask ourselves who can afford to have visions if there's such a cost?

How real can modern life be – is it, as described in the poem 'Paradise Stop', like the inside of the movie made around us? Maybe the issue of loneliness is exemplified in these lines:

Solitude being worse than death,
I remember childhood dreams inside cement.

('Paradise Stop' p. 47)

In the poem 'Avant-gardists', another movie (a Western) expresses the false hope that cannot contain the immensity of contradiction, of the avant-gardist who doesn't have an 'actor's heart', who is a body full of butterflies, who will be sacrificed for challenging the status quo though might find "respect" after they've gone, like the poet Kim Soo-Young. These are references not only to real suffering but also to a sublimated but devastating reality: that of the 1910-1945 Japanese occupation; the division of Korea along the 38th Parallel; the Korean War; the armistice and the 250km long and 4km wide Demilitarised Zone (DMZ) that remains an active "no-man's land" to this day; the fate of the 1960 Students' Revolution; the dictators; the terror of secret police; and the deep trauma of the 1980 "Gwangju Uprising" and mass-murder of citizens ordered by General Chun Doo Hwan. Also woven into the poem are Kim Seung-Hee's rebellion against the social constraints of the 1950s when she was a small child, her awareness of the contradictions of any avant-gardism (which she approaches both with praise *and* irony), the give and take that runs through her work, and the mournful yoked to the celebratory:

> Avant-gardists are dreadfully fierce though they do not mean to be.
> Because they are so lonesome.
> Like the last scene in a western,
> avant-gardists always blow away like the wind,
> like a faint whistle
>
> ('Avant-gardists' p. 49)

Disturbed reassurance is a tonality in Kim Seung-Hee's poetry. Do not think you are safe in the domestic, and do not think the domestic is separate from the world, from nature. In her egg poems (eggs prospectively contain their own navels, which makes for an interesting ontological interiority of self and community on the outside, and other conceptual paradoxes), she is inside the birth, and outside it – the non-birth, the birth, the thwarting, the hope, the ironies. These empathetic but sublaxated poems of "ordinariness" are philosophical meditative inversions, spoken with total "mastery". They blend and move and shift, and create contact points – navels of world:

> I put a bunch of dandelions wrapped in newspaper into the fridge.
> Inside the fridge the dandelions blossom fully,
> white dandelion seeds grow, scatter, find nowhere to go,
> and in the vegetable box spores of white mould form.
> Every time I open the fridge door

>   the spores of white mould left beneath the newspaper as the
>   dandelions rotted
> gradually leak out,
> spread across the kitchen floor,
> get trodden on.
> Foolish dandelions,
> struggle though they may, there are times when they are unable
>   to escape from the fridge.
>
> ('Life in the Egg 7' p. 55)

As we move through Kim Seung-Hee's works we get a sense of the interconnectedness of things and ideas, of the reified and the abstract, of the body and soul, intensifying – her poems build into a complex three-dimensional painting of life, and of the self in the life of (many) communities. So piano and river and *Arirang* [a Korean folk song] can blend contrapuntally, merge and toxify, close yet distant and, in the often contradictory 'release' of the essence of place and being:

> as if stroking your breast's rusty piano with a hand
> after leaping into the filthy Han River
> where embalming fluid mingles with all kinds of poison, blood, rat-killer,
>   and semen,
> then stopping briefly,
> it's hearing far-off a crazy *Arirang* from either side.
>
> ('A Thousand *Arirangs'* – '1 *Piano in the Breast'* p. 61)

I wonder about the pain and stress of sustaining hope, but I know it can be maintained. These are poems of trigger warnings to the self, to be aware, to not let go. I am reminded of Mayakovsky's contradictions between love and disturbed vision in 'A Cloud in Trousers' but tangentially so: Kim Seung-Hee's Korean de-futurism is not waiting for a lover, but moving away from a lover yet remaining divided within:

> At the time not realizing it was love,
> squirming, bygone hours,
> I live with a cloud about my neck.
> If the cloud shakes, my whole body flutters.

My lifeline
is a line hanging from neck to stomach.
Life is right.

('A Thousand *Arirangs*' – '6 *There Is No Book More Lovely than Clay*' p. 69)

In his Preface, Brother Anthony notes scarcity of language-work poems in this selection from two of Kim Seung-Hee's recent volumes of poetry, but he assures us that language is perpetually at play. And through these taut translations we do get a sense of the dexterity and extensions of meaning that are a constant: these "plays" are also aspects of "hope" in that language might generate a way out, even if the word "fails".

Kim Seung-Hee's poetry, as it moves between the actual and conceptual, the concrete and philosophical, works to find ways through. The "chopping board" is the ultimate metaphor of control and loss, of a paradox that doesn't lessen through repetition. Flowers are a vital force of life in her poetry, connecting earth with sun, and the paradox, and maybe its resolution, are found in vibrant (and disturbed) lines such as:

Flowers clamber up onto the chopping board.
Hope being preposterous,
similarly preposterous flowers take their place on the chopping board.

('Cockscomb Time' p. 85)

In her surrealism we see a realignment of the imagistic, of the distilled moment, into discursive questioning: her poems are quite radical in their play with "tradition" in the present. And if travel liberates the mind, it is also a way out of the social constraint of one's personal experience. Kim Seung-Hee seems to search "away" for hope, for other ways of reflecting on where she comes from, and what a broader "we" might be in universal terms. But what she is seeking is not "better" but rather the "unknown", and that unknown is hope. Difference from one's primary lived experience ironically makes hope less lonely. In the poem 'Invitation to a Journey' we read of a visit to America where her daughter lives:

> Drinking an unknown green drink on an unknown street corner,
> going into an unknown bookstore and looking at unknown books,
> then standing with unknown people, each with differently-coloured skin,
> on their way to unknown addresses
> waiting for an unknown bus,
> the freedom of you not knowing them, they not knowing you, is good
> and what is good about the way that freedom is good
> is because you are no more than a scrap of unknown cloud
> with the Hudson River flowing, and that is good.
>
> ('Invitation to a Journey' p. 107)

I find it pertinent that hope resides in the tensions of connection, between different views and maybe "different" Koreas? Towards the end of this volume, in 'Evening's Party', we have an explosion of tension and contradiction, of the fraught history of personal and public violence, of display and interiority, of loss of control and issues of order, of denial and confrontation. We read, against the whirl of evening, the devastating "wounded top has no history"; we read about the sick in the hospital of the world, about the continuing hypocrisy, about the anaesthetising, if not healing, of loneliness as we reach across the pain of history whose nexus solidifies in Gwanghwamun – and throughout echoes the voice of the poet Kim Soo-Young:

> So long as it can love, so long as there is a ray of sunlight,
> so long as the evening's bridge is not cut,
> at the time when it has to heal itself and stand up then stand up again,
>   forever,
> the sick top has no tatty history, no rage, no memory.
>
> ('Evening's Party' p. 121)

The spinning top ("Paengi chigi") is a particularly powerful image in the later poems of this collection: keeping upright and moving "randomly" through the force of the spin, it is a perfect paradox of being. The children spinning their tops become the contradiction of being in the overdetermined place and psychology of social interaction, a sociological poetics. The poem 'A Huge Top' leaves us, in front of the palace gate, with:

> The top is spinning.
> Bright tops are spinning, full of heaven, earth and people.
> As acorns, even squirrels emerge, their bodies shining brightly, the tops
> are spinning.
> Tops made of trees, of swords, of bones, and light,
> the tops are quietly spinning like dreams.
> A huge, huge top, one I cannot even begin to imagine,
> who can distinguish between dream and dreamer, revolution and
> revolutionary?
>
> ('A Huge Top' p. 125)

Here we see both a closeness to and distance from politics, a philosophical rather than a specific politics, the political complexity of these poems residing in the image of the top.

In writing an introduction to a poet I don't personally know, and whose land I have only visited through being stranded in an airport many years ago due to a "crisis", I have tried to connect and converse through many different nodal points (I also have a friend, Dan Disney, a poet and academic who works at the same university as both Kim Seung-Hee and Brother Anthony). Kim Seung-Hee's fascination for the sunflower is vital to me as a way into the affirmations that 'balance', though do not offset, the melancholy; sunflowers are one of the focal points of my life, too, and Ginsberg's 'Sunflower Sutra' is one of my favourite poems.

Kim Seung-Hee's poems speak across lives and out of lives rather than *of* lives, and in this they liberate – women, woman, self, selves, essence from image, life from death. In facing the nuances of an essential poetry and poetics, Brother Anthony's beautiful clarity of line and word allows the complexity of the poems, even with such constant linguistic nuancing and "détournment", to shine through. This poetry, with its shattering lights, brightens the dark places in multiple and intricate ways. It follows the sun, it is of the sun.

John Kinsella

from
HOPE IS LONELY

희망에는 신의 물방울이 들어있다

꽃들이 반짝반짝 했는데
그 자리에 가을이 앉아 있다

꽃이 피어있을 땐 보지 못했던
검붉은 씨가 눈망울처럼 맺혀져 있다

희망이라고....
희망은 직진하진 않지만
희망에는 신의 물방울이 들어 있다

반투명한 불투명

그런 건가? 보이지 않는 건가?
그런 건가? 들리지 않는 건가?
그런 건가? 알지 못하는 건가?
그런 건가? 다 소용없는 건가?
그런 건가? 해가 또 지는 건가?
그런 건가? 이렇게 살다 가라는 건가?
그런 건가? 하루하루 오늘은 괴로움의 나열인데
그런 건가? 띄어쓰기도 없이 범람하며 밀려오는 나날

INSIDE OF HOPE IS GOD'S WATER DROP

Where flowers shone bright
autumn now dominates, instead.

Invisible while the flowers were blooming,
a crimson seed emerges like a water drop.

Hope, now. . . .
Hope does not grow straight
but inside of hope is God's water drop.

TRANSLUCENT OPACITY

Is that it? Is it invisible?
Is that it? Is it inaudible?
Is that it? Is it unknowable?
Is that it? Is it quite useless?
Is that it? Is it the sun setting again?
Is that it? Is it being told to live like this then go?
Is that it? Every day the present day a string of troubles.
Is that it? Days flooding and surging without a break.
Is that it? Is it saying that tomorrow is the same as today?

희망의 연옥

"이 세상은 항상 폐허야. 하지만 우리에겐 작은 기회가 있어. 만약 우리가 아주, 아주 열심히 노력한다면, 우리는 선을 상상할 수 있을 거야. 우리는 파손된 것을 복구할 수 있는 방법들을 생각해낼 수 있어. 조금씩, 조금씩"
(제이 파리니의 〈벤야민의 마지막 횡단〉에서)

그리고 그는 피레네 산맥을 넘어
스페인 작은 마을
안전지대에 도착한 뒤
자살로 생을 마감하였다

이 세상은 항상 그런 최후들로 가득 차 있다
파손된 것들을 복구하는 방법 너머로
가을이 온다
어딘지 그런 절벽들이 푸른 포도밭 과수원 뒤에 아득하다

포도밭 주인은 어디로 갔을까
피레네 산맥을 백번을 넘어도 그 너머 그 너머에도
폐허와 절벽이 가득 차있는 가을 풍경
팔 하나 주면 안잡아 먹지, 눈 하나 주면 안잡아 먹지....
감옥 그너머의 감옥, 절벽 그너머의 절벽, 최후 그너머의 최후
산맥을 넘고 넘어도 산맥
산맥 그너머의 산맥, 절벽 그너머의 절벽, 최후 그너머의 최후
우리는 그런 것을 감옥이라고 부른다
희망의 연옥이라고

그래도라는 섬이 있다

가장 낮은 곳에
젖은 낙엽보다 더 낮은 곳에
그래도라는 섬이 있다
그래도 살아가는 사람들
그래도 사랑의 불을 꺼트리지 않는 사람들

HOPE'S PURGATORY

> *The world is always in disrepair. But we have a little chance, an opportunity.*
> *If we try very, very hard, we can imagine goodness.*
> *We can think of ways to repair the damage, piece by piece.*
>   JAY PARINI, 'Benjamin's Crossing'

So after crossing the Pyrenees
and reaching safety
in a tiny Spanish village,
he ended his life in suicide.

This world is always full of such endings.
Beyond ways of repairing the damage
autumn comes.
Somewhere such cliffs lie, far away, behind green vineyards and orchards.

Where has the owner of the vineyard gone?
Though you cross the Pyrenees one hundred times, crossing, crossing,
autumn landscapes full of ruins and cliffs.
Give an arm, you'll not be butchered. Give an eye, you'll not be butchered. . . .
Prisons beyond prisons, cliffs beyond cliffs, endings beyond endings,
passing mountains, beyond, still mountains,
mountains beyond mountains, cliffs beyond cliffs, endings beyond endings.

We call such things prisons,
hope's purgatory.

THERE'S AN ISLAND CALLED "NEVERTHELESS"

In the lowest place,
lower even than soggy leaves,
there's an island called Nevertheless –
the people who live on Nevertheless
are people who never extinguish the fire of love, nevertheless.

세상에서 가장 아름다운 섬, 그래도
어떤 일이 있더라도
목숨을 끊지 말고 살아야 한다고
천사 같은 김종삼, 박재삼,
그런 착한 마음을 버려선 못쓴다고

부도가 나서 길거리로 쫓겨나고
인기 여배우가 골방에서 목을 메고
뇌출혈로 쓰러져
말 한마디 못해도 가족을 만나면 반가운 마음,
중환자실 환자 옆에서도
힘을 내어 웃으며 살아가는 가족들의 마음속

그런 사람들이 모여 사는 섬, 그래도
그런 사람들이 모여 사는 섬, 그래도
그 가장 아름다운 것 속에
더 아름다운 피묻은 이름,
그 가장 서러운 것 속에 더 타오르는 찬란한 꿈
누구나 다 그런 섬에 살면서도
세상의 어느 지도에도 알려지지 않은 섬,
그래서 더 신비한 섬,
그래서 더 가꾸고 싶은 섬, 그래도
그대 가슴속의 따스한 미소와 장미빛 체온
이글이글 사랑의 눈이 부신 영광의 함성

그래도라는 섬에서
그래도 부둥켜안고
그래도 손만 놓지 않는다면
언젠가 강을 다 건너 빛의 뗏목에 올라서리라,
어디엔가 걱정 근심 다 내려놓은 평화로운
그래도, 거기에서 만날 수 있으리라

The most beautiful island in the world – Nevertheless,
insisting that, no matter what happens,
one must go on living, not terminate life,
one must never cast aside hearts kind like those
of the angel-like poets Kim Jong-Sam or Park Jae-Sam.

Bankrupt and thrown out onto the street;
a popular star who hanged herself in a backroom;
someone who has suffered a stroke,
unable to speak, still glad at heart on meeting family
in an intensive care ward,
in the heart of the family, bravely smiling, going on with life

The island where that kind of people gather, Nevertheless,
the island where people like that gather nevertheless,
and within that most beautiful thing,
bloodstained, a yet more beautiful name,
in that most sorrowful thing an even more radiant dream blazing,
and although any and every one lives on such an island,
it's an island that's not marked on any map of the world.
Therefore a more mysterious island,
therefore an island I long even more to cultivate, Nevertheless,
a warm smile, rose-tinted warmth within your heart,
a cry of glory, dazzling with blazing love.

On the island called Nevertheless,
if you embrace nevertheless,
so long as you do not lose hold, nevertheless,
one day we will cross over the river and step onto a raft of light,
and somewhere, on that peaceful Nevertheless,
cares and worries set aside,
there, we'll finally meet.

하얀 접시에 올라온 하얀 가자미 한 마리

나는
'나는'이라든가 '내가'라든가 하는
말을 잊어야만 한다고
또한 '나의'라든가 '내'라든가 하는 말도 다 버려야만 한다고
바다처럼 푸른 식탁보가 깔린
작은 나무 식탁 앞에서
하얀 접시에 올라온 하얀 가자미 한 마리를 보면서
문득 생각나는 것이다

이 은은하고 도도한 광채어린, 이 접시는 나에게 속삭인다
흰 살 가자미의 껍질, 지느러미, 빼낸 창자, 형제 자매, 부모, 고향
그런 것을 다 복원해 낼 수 있는가,
내가 주어가 될 수 없다는 것
나의 소유격도 결국은 다 파도거품처럼 무의미하다는 것
그렇다면 여기서는 접시가 주어란 말인가?
푸른 칼자루가, 모래밭이 주어란 말인가?
오른쪽으로 두 눈이 쏠려있는 가자미
껍질을 다 벗기우고 하얀 살만 접시 위에 올라와 있다
희망의 현실적 근거가 하나도 없지 않은가?
희망이란 원래 그런 것이 아닌가?
갈 데까지 다 간 마음....
접시에 대한 좌절, 몸부림, 굴종이 오고
이 시대에 누가 장편 소설, 대하 소설을 쓰는가?
있는 것은 몽따쥬, 토막토막 단상 밖에는,
이 은은하고도 도도한 광채
접시 하나가 세계 전체와 맞먹는 일일 수도
전혀 아름답지 않은 이 접시 위의 몰락
외부는 언제나 파괴적인 힘으로
우리에게 관여한다
이 하얀 접시 앞에 놓인 나이프와 포크
앞의 신경증

그런 식으로 그 날 별이 칼집난 내 가슴에 소롯이 들어왔다

ONE WHITE FLATFISH LYING ON A WHITE DISH

I
think we must forget words
such as "I" or "myself,"
I think we must give up words like "my" and "mine."
Before a small wooden table
covered with a sea-blue tablecloth,
seeing the remains of one white flatfish on a white dish,
the thought suddenly strikes me.

This dish, delicate and proud, brilliant, is whispering to me:
That white-fleshed flatfish, its skin and fins, the guts removed, brothers,
                                                      sisters, parents, home,
can you restore all those?
The way I cannot become a subject,
the way my possessives are all ultimately meaningless like the foam on a wave,
does that mean then that here the dish is the subject,
that the blue knife-handle, the sandbank, are subjects?
The flatfish with both eyes twisted to the right,
its skin all stripped off, lies on the white dish as mere pieces of white flesh.
Is there really not one realistic ground for hope?
Isn't that basically what hope is?
A heart that has gone as far as it can . . . .
Frustration, agony, surrender concerning the dish arrive
and these days does anyone write full-length novels or sagas?
Everything is nothing but montage, fragments of a platform,
This delicate, proud brilliance,
this one dish may be equivalent to the world as a whole.
The most unlovely wreckage on this dish,
the outside ever involves us
with destructive power.
The knife and fork placed before this white dish,
frontal neurosis.

In that way that day's star slipped slyly into my slashed breast.

말은 울고 있다

말은 울고 있다
제 무능을 울고 있다
말은 모든 것이지만
말은 아무 것도 아니다
말은 울고 있다
소리 없이 울고 있다
소리 소리 소리 소리 뿐이다
소리 소리 소리 뿐일까?
덧없음의 소리의 물 위의 가면무도회다
모네의 수련 위에 떨어지는 햇빛이다
물안개 속에 감싸인 나체의 수련이다
빙글빙글 휘돌아 나가는 소용돌이의 현기증이다
익사했을 때 말은 가면을 벗는다
말의 속살이 복숭아처럼 화안하다
몽유도원도에 말은 없지만 또 말은 복숭아처럼 가득하다
복숭아처럼 가득한 말은 말의 피안에 있다
잡을 수가 없다 형용할 수도 없다
말은 아무 것도 아닌 것이다
말은 미끌어진다
말은 모든 것의 피안이며 아무 것의 피안이다
나는 울고 있다
나는 나인데
네가 아니고 나인데
모든 것이며 아무 것도 아니며
말의 기원도 아니며
말 보다 뒤에 물결의 흔적처럼 나타나는 자
허무이자 피안이다

향그리움.... 언어의 항아리다

A WORD IS WEEPING

A word is weeping.
It is weeping over its own incompetence.
A word is everything but
a word is nothing.
A word is weeping.
Without a sound, it is weeping.
Nothing but sound, sound, sound.
Is it really only sound, sound, sound?
It's a masquerade on the waters of frailty's sound.
It's sunlight falling on Monet's water-lilies.
It's naked water-lilies wrapped in mist.
It's the vertigo of a spinning, turning, eddying whirlpool.
When it's drowned, a word removes its mask.
A word's flesh is luscious like a peach.
The painting 'Dream Journey to the Peach Blossom Land' has no words
but still a word is full like a peach.
A word full like a peach has reached a word's world beyond.
It is incomprehensible. It is indescribable.
A word is nothing.
A word is slippery.
A word is everything's other world and nothing's other world.
I am weeping.
I am I,
not you but I,
everything and nothing,
not a word's origin,
someone appearing after a word like the trace of a wave,
the void and the world beyond.

Fragrance. . . . the storage-pot of language.

자유인의 꿈

자유인....
그건 오해야,

땅 끝에서 바다를, 바다의 끝에서 하늘을
그렇게 도화지를 다 지워버렸다고,
처음인양 푸른 파도, 흰 구름, 갈매기를 바라보고 있다고

그건 오해야,
홀로 가는 구름은, 새는, 파도는 자유를 어쩌지 못해

자유는 그런 데서 오지 않더라,
죄의 깡통을 들고 피를 빌어먹더라,

장터에서 지는 싸움을 다 싸우고
시선으로 포위된 땡볕, 장마당 한복판에
피 흘리는 심장을 내려놓았을 때
징 소리가 울리고
막이 내리고
그런 패배를 견뎌야 자유인이 되더라

소금을 뚫고
꿈,
미친년의 머리에 꽂은 꽃 같은 거더라

매화는 힘이 세다

다른 것은 몰라도
저 얼음덩어리 빙하의 땅 밑에는
곰이 겨울잠을 자고
죽은 유리디체를 찾아 오르페우스가 간 길이
구비구비 있을 것이다,

DREAM OF SOMEONE FREE

Someone free. . . .
That's a misunderstanding.

The sea at the land's end, the sky at the sea's end,
I say I erased all that from the drawing paper.
I say I am gazing as though for the first time at blue waves,
                              white clouds, seagulls.

That's a misunderstanding.
Clouds, birds, waves, moving alone, cannot equal freedom.

Freedom never comes there.
Carrying a can of sin, begging blood to eat

After fighting all the fights on the market-place,
bright sunlight hemmed in by eyes, as I lay down a bleeding heart
in the middle of the market square
the jing booms out,
the curtain falls,
only by enduring such defeats can you become free.

Piercing salt,
a dream,
it's like the flower perched on a crazy woman's head.

PLUM BLOSSOM IS MIGHTY

Not sure about other things,
but under that mass of ice and the frozen ground
a bear is sleeping its winter sleep
and the path Orpheus took in search of dead Eurydice
will go winding down.

겨울잠을 자는 곰보다도 못한 것이
인간이다.
인간은 부스럭댄다,
그 인간보다도 못한 것이 저승의 악사다
빙하를 뚫고 저승으로 길 떠난 오르페우스다
죽음을 우는, 죽음을 살리려는 오르페우스다
살리지 못하였다
유리디체는 이미 죽었고 다시한번 또 죽었다
강물이 풀리면
그 물 위로 오르페우스의 머리와 수금이 둥둥 떠내려 간다
그 혼이 피기 전에 매화가 핀다

매화는 힘이 세다

바람을 옷에 싼 여자

여자,
바람을 옷으로 싸고
물을 보자기로 모으는 여자,
해와 별을 가슴에 기르고
정액과 피를 모아
(아, 너로구나, 너였구나. . . .)
그것은 바람의 연애, 사람을 태어나게 한 여자

두 손으로 바람을 모아
뼈와 근육과 신경과 골수를 짜넣은 여자
영혼을 살로 싼 여자
심장 속에 절대로 꺼지지 않는 불을 넣은 여자
언제나 위험 보다 더 위험하고
허무 보다 더 허무하고
시간 보다 더 덧없는 여자

A human being
is even more helpless than a hibernating bear.
Humans rustle.
Even more helpless than a human is that otherworldly musician,
Orpheus, who pierced the ice and set off for the other world,
Orpheus who lamented death, who wanted to bring death to life.
He failed.
Eurydice had already died, then she died again.
When the river melts,
on the water Orpheus's head and lyre will go floating down.
Before his spirit blossoms, plum trees will blossom.

Plum blossom is mighty.

WOMAN WRAPPING THE WIND IN CLOTHES

Woman,
wrapping the wind in clothes,
woman gathering up water with a wrapping cloth,
woman raising sun and stars at your breast,
mingling semen and blood
(ah, you, it was you)
that was the wind's love, bringing humans to birth.

Woman who gathered the wind with both hands,
then wove together bones and muscles and nerves and marrow;
woman who wrapped soul in flesh;
woman who set in the heart a flame that will never be extinguished,
woman always more dangerous than danger,
emptier than emptiness,
more transient than time.

두 손에 모은 바람은 흐터지고
보자기로 싼 물은 흘러 떨어지고
살에 새겨 넣은 혼은 날아가고
숨결로 구름을 만들어도
절대로 꺼지지 않는 불을 심장 속에 간직한
이 여자, 인류 대대로 바람을 옷으로 싼 여자,

여자가 낳은 것

여자가 낳은 것마다
물이 되어버리고
여자가 낳은 것마다 바람이 되어버리니
그럼 여자는 물을 낳은 것인가, 바람을 낳은 것인가
여자가 낳은 것은 뼈이고 흙일뿐인가

바람의 어머니
물의 어머니
뼈의 어머니
흙의 어머니

보아라, 순간에서 순간까지
이슬에서 이슬까지
여자가 낳은 것이 하늘 아래 가장 좋은 것이면서
여자가 낳은 것이
또 하늘 아래 가장 아픈 것

The wind gathered in both hands scatters,
the water gathered in a wrapping cloth falls and flows away,
the soul inscribed in flesh flies away,
and though this woman makes clouds with her breath,
she has in her heart a flame that will never be extinguished,
as, generation after generation, she robes the wind in clothes.

WHAT WOMEN GIVE BIRTH TO

Everything women give birth to
turns into water;
everything women give birth to turns into wind;
So is it water or wind that women give birth to?
Is what women give birth to nothing but bone and clay?

Mother of wind,
mother of water,
mother of bone,
mother of clay.

See, from moment to moment,
from dew to dew,
what women give birth to is the best thing under heaven
and what women give birth to
is the most painful thing under heaven.

시의 응급실에서

시는 응급실, 시는 산소텐트, 시는 시린 사과 속의 빨간 피,
슬픔은 비료와 같아
시의 이곳저곳에 뿌려둬야지,
시는 임산부의 날
언제가 해산의 날인지 아무도 알지 못하는 날,
시는 폭탄을 안고 달린다,
구름 위로 달린다,
그런데 다랑논 하나만한 논에서
누런 벼들이 익어가고 있다,
밥 한 공기만한 논, 삿갓으로 덮어도 될 만큼
작은 한 공기의 삿갓 논,
죽그릇, 밥그릇 하나만한 죽배미, 밥배미,
삿갓배미여,
무릇 환자는 죽 한 그릇으로 원기소성하노니
가을 다랑논 한 배미의 힘으로
나를 살리고 너를 살려
다시 논에 엎드려 언어의 이삭을 줍고
언어의 씨앗을 심게 하나니
층층이 겹쳐진 황금빛 다랑논
당신의 시 한 편
김이 펄펄 나는 밥 한 공기 당신의 서정시 전집

모래 거울

대체 거울에게 무얼 물어보려는 거야?

그만 둬,

세상의 모든 거울은 모래로 만들어져 있다네,

IN POETRY'S EMERGENCY ROOM

Poetry is emergency room, poetry is oxygen tent, poetry is red blood
                                        inside a cold apple,
sorrow is like fertilizer
that must be sprinkled here and there on poetry,
poetry is a pregnant woman's day,
the day of delivery: nobody knows when it will be;
poetry comes racing embracing a bomb,
racing over the clouds.
Yet in one tiny paddy-field,
yellow heads of rice are ripening.
A field the size of a bowl of rice, small enough for a conical hat to cover,
a tiny bowl of a hat-field,
a gruel-bowl sized, rice-bowl sized gruel-field, rice-field,
hat-field.
Ordinary patients recover energy thanks to a bowl of gruel,
so by the power of a small strip of autumnal paddy
I am saved, you are saved,
so once again we lie flat on the field gleaning ears of language
then sow seeds of language
so that golden paddy-fields rise in tiers,
one of your poems,
a steaming bowl of rice, your collection of lyric poems.

SAND MIRROR

What on earth are you asking the mirror?

Stop it!

Why, all the mirrors in the world are made of sand.

거울 안에 꽃이 피었다고
거울 안에 비누 거품 향기가 보름달의 말을 할 때도
거울의 말을 듣는 것이 음악처럼 아름다울 때라도

한 시간

두 시간

거울의 편지를 뜯지는 마

세상의 모든 거울은 모래로 만들어져 있으니까

정치는 그 사회의 거울이다
시는 그 사회의 거울이다
꿈은 슬픔의 거울이다

왜 거울은 모래로 만들어졌을까?

보헤미안 유리 거울

모래밭에 이름을 묻고

떠나기, 환상이라는 거울이 깨져 흩어진 모래만 남은,

얼굴이 없는 신체만 남은, 시간이 사라져 시계만 남은....

흰 잠옷을 뒤집어쓴 채 강에 빠져 죽었다는 어느 화가의 어머니

흰 잠옷으로 가려진 얼굴

거울에서 손이 나와 자꾸만 모래를 눈에 뿌리네

모래 거울

영혼이 없는 대답이라네

Flowers were said to have bloomed in mirrors.
Even when soap-bubble-like perfume spoke the full moon's words in the mirror,
even when listening to the mirror's words is beautiful like music.

One hour.

Two hours.

Do not open the mirror's letter.

Since all the mirrors in the world are made of sand.

Politics is society's mirror.
Poetry is society's mirror.
A dream is sorrow's mirror.

Why are mirrors made of sand?

A Bohemian glass mirror,

asked its name in a sandy field,

went away, a mirror called illusions shattering, only scattered sand left,

only a faceless body left, time vanishing, only a clock left. . . .

an artist's mother said to have died after falling into a river wrapped
                                                in white pyjamas

a face veiled by white pyjamas.

A hand emerges from the mirror, keeps sprinkling sand in the eyes.

Sand mirror.

That is an answer without a soul.

낙원 역

이것은 영화다....
이런 생각을 한다
이런 생각을 하는 한
고통은 나의 고통이 아니다
핸들을 놓아버리면 죽겠지....
절망은 나의 신경이자 핏줄
절망은 자폭을 향해 간다
강변도로를 달리며 시나리오를 넘기듯이 생각한다

이것은 영화다....
그런 생각을 하는 한
절망은 나의 절망이 아니다
욕망이라는 이름의 전차에 올라
'묘지'로 갈아탄 다음 '낙원' 역에서 내리세요....
어느 영화에서 들은 말이다
영화 제목은 잊어버렸는데 마치 그 주인공이 자기 같다

영화를 찍는다고 생각하면
오늘이 오늘이 아니고
자기는 자기가 아니고
내일은 내일의 태양이 뜨겠지요....
절망엔 비약이 있다
폐허에 내일의 태양이 떠오른다
손에 흙을 쥐고 내일, 내일, 내일.... 고향으로 돌아간다고 말하는
붉은 여왕, 흙의 딸

이것은 영화다....
생각하는 동안
해가 지고 해가 뜨고
흰 건반이 검은 건반이 되고 검은 건반이 흰 건반이 되고
집도 절도 없이
둘 사이는 멀어지고 멍하고 멍멍하고
고통은 타인의 고통
주인공은 늘 고난에 처하지만 사랑을 독려한다

PARADISE STOP

This is a movie. . . .
That's what I am thinking.
In thinking that,
pain is not my pain.
If I let go of the wheel I'll die. . . .
Despair is my nerves, my veins,
despair heads toward suicide bombing.
As I speed along the riverside highway,
I am thinking as if skimming through a scenario.

This is a movie. . . .
In thinking like that,
despair is not my despair.
Board a streetcar named desire,
then after changing at 'Cemetery' get off at 'Paradise'. . . .
I heard that in some movie.
I've forgotten its name but the star was just like you, dear.

When I think I'm shooting a movie
today is not today,
you are not you,
tomorrow tomorrow's sun will rise for sure. . . .
There's rapid growth in despair.
Tomorrow's sun is rising amid ruins.
Clay grasped in its hands, tomorrow, tomorrow, tomorrow. . . . saying:
                                        I'm going back home,
the Red Queen, clay's daughter.

This is a movie. . . .
while I'm thinking that
the sun sets, the sun rises,
the white keys turn into black keys, the black keys turn into white keys,
with nothing to call their own,
they move further apart, stupefied, deafened,
pain is someone else's pain,
the star always gets into trouble, but encourages love.

죽음 보다 고독이 더 무서워
시멘트 속에서 어린 시절의 꿈을 생각하네

심장이 총알에 뚫렸을 때도 죽지 않는다
총알 구멍 사이로 파란 하늘을 본다
이것은 영화다....

전위의 사람

전위의 사람들은 대개 총을 맞고 먼저 죽는다
몸속에 수천 마리 나비가 날아다녀서일 것이다
산다는 것이 조금 비굴하다고 느껴지는 때가 있다
밥 먹고 사는 일에 문제가 생겼을 때다
밥을 안먹고 살면 되지 않을까,
김수영도 푼돈을 벌려고 번역거리를 해서 잡지사에 가 앉아서
편집자들에게 당신이 일해 오는 것을 보면 무섭다는 둥
그런 모욕, 희롱, 고통의 말을 듣기도 했다지만
전위의 사람들이 총을 맞고 죽으면 멋있지만
배우처럼 등을 바꾸고 살면 비굴이다
배우는 앞으로도 뒤로도 등을 바꿀 수가 있다
전위의 사람들은 몸으로 온몸으로 나비를 해야 한다
비눗방울을 해야 한다
봐라, 나비 날개는 너덜거리고
비눗방울은 선풍기 날개에 부딪쳐 찢어진다
선풍기의 앞과 뒤는 완전히 다르다
폭포수 같은 바람이 돌지 않는 것이다
선풍기는 앞과 뒤를 확연히 끊어놓는다
전위의 사람은 미래를 향해서 선풍기의 회전 속으로
곧추 떨어져야 한다
절대로 배우의 마음으로 살아서는 안된다
일회성이라는 금선 위에 서야 한다
용기에는 유보나 반복이 있어서는 안된다, 선택은

Solitude being worse than death,
I remember childhood dreams inside cement.

Even when the heart is pierced by a bullet,
through the bullet hole the blue sky is visible.
This is a movie. . . .

AVANT-GARDISTS

Usually avant-gardists are shot and killed first,
probably because they have thousands of butterflies flying about inside them.
There are times when saying I'm alive feels obsequious.
It's when a problem arises about eating and living.
Would it not be all right to live without eating?
Just as Kim Soo-Young, having done some translations to earn pocket money,
went and sat down in a magazine publisher's office,
where he was told by the editors, 'We feel afraid when we see you working',
and heard that kind of insult, ridicule, painful words,
so if avant-gardists are shot and killed, that's cool,
but if they live like actors changing lamps, that's servile.
An actor can change lamps forwards and backwards.
Avant-gardists have to be butterflies with their bodies, their whole bodies.
They have to be soap-bubbles.
Only look, butterfly wings are tattered.
If soap-bubbles hit the wings of a fan they burst.
The front and back of a fan are utterly different.
Wind like a waterfall is something that does not turn.
It clearly separates the front and back of a fan.
Avant-gardists have to face the future then fall straight
into a fan's revolutions.
They absolutely must not live with an actor's heart.
They have to stand on the gold thread known as a one-off.

하나의 자살이라고
전위의 사람은 의도하지 않아도 지독하게 냉엄하다
허허롭기 때문이다
서부영화의 마지막 장면처럼
전위의 사람은 언제나 바람처럼 떠난다
가느다란 휘파람 소리가
하늘과 땅의 한가운데를 살짝 파란 나이프로 긋고 가는 것처럼
전위의 사람은 떠날 때까지
온몸 속에 나비가 가득 살아있는 사람
무지갯빛 비눗방울로 앞으로 점점 춤추는 사람

달걀 속의 생 6

달걀은 여전히 냉장고 위 칸에 희고 얌전히 꽂혀져 있다,
시간의 연옥,
똑똑똑 떨어지는 물시계 소리,
기다림 없는 기다림으로
채소에서 우거지로
냉장고 문을 열면 언제나 달걀은
은은한 눈초리로 나를 바라본다
내가 순간 환한 피사체가 된다

너 아직 살아 있었구나.... 고운 달걀이여
인생은 얼마나 울퉁불퉁한데
인생은 각목 같은 것인데
아직 그 고운 껍질 아래 두근두근 일기를 쓰는 달걀이 있다
숨결의 적층이 달걀의 일기라면
달빛 서리처럼 숨결은 하얗고 차갑게 퍼져가고
알알이
어룽대면서 아.... 라고 하나.... 어... 라고.... 우.... 라고나,
오선지 아래 가리워진 마음
아우라지 강가에서 말문을 못 열고

There must be no reserves or repetition in courage. Choice
is seen as a form of suicide
Avant-gardists are dreadfully fierce though they do not mean to be.
Because they are so lonesome.
Like the last scene in a western,
avant-gardists always blow away like the wind,
like a faint whistle
drawing a line between heaven and earth with a very sharp knife,
people living with bodies full of butterflies,
people slowly dancing ahead as rainbow-hued soap-bubbles,
until avant-gardists go away.

LIFE IN THE EGG 6

As ever, an egg is meekly lodged on the top shelf of the fridge.
Time's purgatory,
the *drip drip drip* of a water clock.
With an unexpectant expectancy
from greens to cabbage leaves
whenever I open the door of the fridge
the egg gazes at me delicately.
I briefly become a bright subject for a photo.

You're still alive. . . . lovely egg!
Human life is so bumpy,
human life is like lumber
yet still within that lovely shell, palpitating, there's an egg keeping a diary.
If layers of breath are the egg's diary,
like moonlight frost, the breath spreads white and chill,
airy,
speckled, saying "a". . . . or "o". . . . or "u",
the heart screened beneath a sheet of stave paper
unable to speak by a river where two streams blend,

입김으로 어리던 어룽거림. . . . 하얀 서리

말문을 못 열고, 알알이. . . . 알영. . . . 아리영. . . .
아리랑이었을까. . . .
규원가여, 채련곡, 봄비를 쓰던 날의 난설헌 말고
규원가를 쓰던 밤의. . . . 난설헌이여,
"봄바람 가을 물이 뵈오리. . . . 내 얼굴 내 보거니
. . . . 스스로 참괴하니 누구를 원망하리"
얼굴이 점점 메말라 가며
일그러진 진주여, 뼈까지 시들어가는 병든 야채여
"푸른 난새는 채색 난새에 기대었구나.
부용꽃 스물일곱 송이가 붉게 떨어지니
달빛 서리 위에서 차갑기만 해라."
어느 날 「몽유광상산시」를 쓰고
그리고 마침내 「유선사」를 썼네

「유선사」 속에서 그녀는 붉은 얼굴로 부용봉 언덕을 뛰어 오르고
산을 오르고 향기로운 술을 마시고 붓으로 편지를 쓰고
신선을 만나 사랑하고 채색 구슬을 가지고 놀고
채색 난새를 타고 달빛 서리 위를 뛰어 올랐다,
몽유를 타고 유선사를 쓰던 난설헌이 나는 좋았지만
냉장고 속에 부용꽃
부용꽃 스물일곱 송이가 붉게 꽃피었다 떨어지고
몸서리치는 서리꽃이여
나의 지문으로 서리꽃을 문질러 데워보지만
그것은 단지 사랑의 역설

한 노래가 냉장고를 떠매고
한 세상 밖으로 느릿느릿 나아간다
아는 얼굴들이 고개를 넘는 이야기
아우라지 강가에서 속삭이는 애절함

speckles formed by breath. . . . white frost

Unable to speak, airy. . . . raining. . . . raining. . . .
or was it *Arirang*? . . . .
Ah, that song, *Gyuwon-ga, Chaeryon-gog*, not a song written by
                                                 Nanseolheon on a rainy day
but written one rainy night. . . . ah, Nanseolheon!
"I see spring breezes, autumn waters. . . . I see my face reflected
 . . . . weird in itself, who should I blame?"
Faces slowly drying out,
distorted pearls, even the bones withering, sick vegetables,
"A blue luan bird was leaning against a grey luan bird.
Twenty-seven rose mallows wither red
on moonlight frost so sense the chill."
One day she wrote 'Strolling over Mulberry Mountain in a Dream',
then finally 'Wandering Still'.

In 'Wandering Still' she goes running up Buyong Peak with flushed face,
then once at the summit she drinks fragrant wine and writes a letter,
meets and makes love with a mountain hermit, plays with green beads,
mounts on the back of a green luan bird, goes running across moonlight frost.
I used to like Nanseolheon who wrote 'Wandering Still' in her sleep,
but the rose mallows in the fridge,
the twenty-seven rose mallow flowers
you frost-flowers, shuddering, blossoming red, withering,
I erase the frost-flowers with the heat of my fingerprints
but that is merely love's paradox.

One song hoists the fridge onto its shoulder
and slowly bears it out of the world.
There are tales of familiar faces climbing over a pass,
sorrow whispering by a river where two streams blend,

[*Nanseolheon:* Heo Nanseolheon (1563–1589) was a famous Korean female poet.]

아리랑 고개를 넘어가는 이야기가 있고
못 넘어가고 시들다가 죽어간 이야기도 있는데
똑똑똑 떨어지는 물시계 소리 아래
인생이 너무 추워서
달걀의 일기는 끝도 없이 계속 된다

달걀 속의 생 7

네? 저, 이번에도 삼송 냉장고 샀어요,
네? 냉장고.... 도어 타입은 양문형이고요
문 색깔은 루비에 하얀 펄이 반짝이는 것인데요,
아름다워요, 요즈음 냉장고 문은 모네의 캔버스 같아요,
문이 많다고 도망갈 길이 많은 건 아니죠,
피 묻은 캔버스에 하얀 눈이 펄펄 내리는 것 같죠,
양쪽으로 여니까 편리해요,
내부도 깨끗하고 넓게 보이고요,
냉장고 속이 아니라 환한 무대 같다니까요,
헤밍웨이의「깨끗하고 불빛 밝은 곳」이라는 단편을 읽은 적이 있죠,
한 노인이 너무 외로워서 밤늦도록
깨끗하고 불빛이 밝은 카페를 찾는 이야기,
노인은 엊그제 밧줄로 목을 맸는데 조카딸이 풀어줬다죠,
젊은 웨이터는 노인이 귀찮아
당신은 지난주에 자살을 했었어야 한다고 말하지만
늙은 노인은 귀머거리라 알아듣지 못하죠,
뭘 드릴까요? 바텐더가 묻자
허무
하고 대답해요,
바텐더는 생각해요,
또 미친 사람이군....
허무가 두려워
깨끗하고 불빛이 밝은 곳을 찾는 사람들

tales of climbing over Arirang Pass,
as well as tales that could not climb over but withered and died
while beneath the water clock's *drip drip drip*
life being too cold,
the egg's diary continues, endless.

LIFE IN THE EGG 7

What? Yes, I bought another Samsong fridge.
What? Fridge. . . . the type with double doors.
It's ruby coloured with glitter sparkling in it,
it looks lovely; nowadays fridge doors are like Monet's canvases.
Lots of doors means lots of ways to escape, right?
It's like white snow falling on a bloodstained canvas.
It opens either way, that's convenient
Inside it looks clean and spacious,
more like a bright stage than the inside of a fridge
You've read Hemingway's 'A Clean, Well-Lighted Place' haven't you?
About an old man who is lonely so he stays sitting
in a clean, well-lighted cafe until late at night.
He tried to hang himself a few days before, his niece cut him down,
the young waiter is annoyed at the old man,
tells him "You should have killed yourself last week,"
but the old man is deaf, does not understand him.
"What's yours?" asks the barman.
"*Nada*," comes the reply
"*Otro loco mas*," says the barman.
People visit clean, well-lighted places
because they fear nothing.

[*Samsong* is a deliberate mis-spelling]

"허무에 계신 우리들의 허무이시여, 그대 이름은 허무이시다"

밝고 깨끗한 곳으로 말하자면 냉장고만큼
밝고 깨끗한 곳은 없죠,
냉장고는 가급적 싱싱한 현재를 지향하죠,
허무가 두려운
세상의 여름과 야채는 냉장고 속으로 다 들어가죠,
삼송 냉장고 안에 당신의 갈구의 모든 것이 들어가요,
목이 마르고
목이 마르고
목이 마를수록 냉장고는 점점 더 커가고
가난하고
가난하고
가난할수록 사람들은 더 깨끗하고 밝은 불빛에 의존적이 되죠,
썩어서 허무가 되는 것이 두려워서요,
캄캄한 육체의 밤이 두려워서요,

민들레 한 단을 신문지에 싸서 냉장고에 두었어요,
삼송 냉장고 안에 민들레가 가득 피고
하얀 민들레 씨앗은 만발하여 흩어져 어디로 갈 줄을 몰라
야채 칸 속에 하얀 곰팡이 홀씨로 맺혀 있어요,
냉장고 문을 열 때마다
신문지 아래서 민들레 한단이 썩어 남긴 하얀 홀씨들이 조금씩 새나와
거실 바닥으로 밀려다녀요,
거실 바닥 발바닥에 밟히며
바보 민들레
아무리 발버둥 쳐도 냉장고 안을 벗어나지 못하는 시간이 있죠

"Our *nada* who art in *nada*, *nada* be thy name,"

When it comes to clean, well-lighted places,
there's nothing as clean and well-lighted as a fridge.
The aim of a fridge is a present as cool as can be.
Fearing *nada*,
the world's summer and veg all make their way into the fridge.
All your cravings make their way into the fridge.
The thirstier,
the thirstier,
the thirstier you are, the bigger the fridge grows;
the poorer,
the poorer,
the poorer people get, the more they grow dependent on clean,
                                              bright lamplight.
Because they fear whatever rots and turns to nothing.
They fear the dark night of the flesh.

I put a bunch of dandelions wrapped in newspaper into the fridge.
Inside the fridge the dandelions blossom fully,
white dandelion seeds grow, scatter, find nowhere to go,
and in the vegetable box spores of white mould form.
Every time I open the fridge door
the spores of white mould left beneath the newspaper as the
                                              dandelions rotted
gradually leak out,
spread across the kitchen floor,
get trodden on.
Foolish dandelions,
struggle though they may, there are times when they are unable to
                                              escape from the fridge.

달걀 속의 생 8

달걀을 던지지 마라

오히려 달걀이 돌이 되어가는 시간을 기다려라

달걀이 돌이 되어가는 시간이 있다
달걀이 물이 되어가는 시간도 있다
돌 보다 작은 다윗의 조약돌이 되어가는 시간이 있다
아무리 발버둥 쳐도 삼송 냉장고 안을 벗어나지 못하는 시간이 있다
돌이 달걀의 안에서 팽창해가는 시간이 있다
수축해 가는 시간도 있다

그러저러한 어느 봄, 부활의 날을 기다려서

세상의 모든 달걀들아, 궐기하라,
양계장에서 도매상 창고에서 수퍼마켓 진열대에서 집집마다 냉장고에서
세상의 모든 달걀들아
궐기하라. . . .
깃발이 없어도
노오란 봄에 불현듯 피어나는
방향이 없어도 우후죽순 같이
노오란 개나리꽃처럼 궐기하라

잠옷을 입은 채로라도 광화문 네거리에서 만나
노란 털이 조금 보이는 피 묻은 이마로라도
서로 꿈을 훔쳐보며
날아가는 달걀은 어차피 허무주의적 깃발!

LIFE IN THE EGG 8

Don't throw eggs.

Better wait until the egg has turned into a stone.

There's a time when an egg turns into a stone.
There's also a time when an egg turns into water.
There's a time when it turns into a little David pebble rather than a stone.
There are times when it is unable to escape from inside a fridge,
struggle though it may.
There are times when a stone expands inside an egg.
And times when it contracts.

On such and such a spring day, having awaited the day of resurrection . . .

All you eggs of the world, arise!
In poultry farms, in wholesale warehouses, in supermarket display stands,
in the fridges in every house,
all you eggs of the world,
arise. . . .
even without banners,
like yellow forsythia
suddenly blooming yellow in spring,
springing up with no particular direction, arise.
Even in pyjamas, encountered at Gwanghwamun crossing,
even with a bloodstained brow showing traces of yellow down,
in any case eggs that go flying off
glancing at each other's dreams, are nihilistic banners!

천의 아리랑

   1. 가슴 속의 피아노

누구나 한번은 떨어지고 싶어 한강으로 간다,
가슴에 검은 피아노 한 대를 질질 끌고
한강 다리를 취중 횡단....
야, 이 미친 년(놈)아, 너 죽고싶어?
흠뻑 쌍욕을 먹어본 적이 있다,죽고 싶으면 저나 혼자.... 환장....
뒷통수에 따라오는 빛나는 쌍욕의 훈장을 끌고 강가에 서면

그런 떨어지는 것들이 모두 모여 강물이 숨을 쉰다,
이렇게 많은 피아노들이 한강에 떨어졌는가,
달을 주렁주렁 매달고 미친 피아노들이 숨을 쉰다,
강물은 숨결, 숨결은 이야기, 누군가의 숨결, 산맥의 이야기,
오늘밤에도 누군가
한강 물 속에서 녹슬고 부서진 벅찬 피아노의 탄식을 듣는다,

사랑이란 그렇게 시작되는 것이다,
나의 가슴 안에 있는 아리랑이
너의 가슴 안에 있는 아리랑을 알아보는 것이다,
1890년대 후반 이자벨 버드 비숍 여사는 4번의 조선 여행 중에 알아보았다,
조선 백성들의 존재 이유는
오직 피를 빨아먹는 흡혈귀들에게 피를 공급하는 것뿐이라고,
아리랑이 있었고 아리랑은 명사가 아니라
동사요
서로 가시를 내밀어 부비며 쑤시며 마구 찔렸어도
다만 흘러내리는 피가 더웠기 때문이다

사랑이란 그런 것이다,
너의 가슴 안에 있는 아리랑이

A THOUSAND *ARIRANGS*

1 PIANO IN THE BREAST

Everybody heads once for the Han River, wanting to fall in.
Dragging a piano in their breast
across the Han River Bridge in a drunken state. . . .
everyone has experienced being cursed out:
Hey, are you crazy? Do you want to die?
If you want to die, you can manage alone. . . . crazy. . . .
standing on the river bank wearing glorious curse-medals
pinned to the back of your head.

Gathering together all those falling things, the river breathes.
Have so many pianos really fallen into the Han River?
Hanging up clustered moons, crazy pianos breathe.
The river is breath, the breath is speech, someone's breath, mountains' speech.
Tonight, too, someone
is listening to the sighs of all those pianos submerged, rusting and
                                                  broken in the Han River.

That's how love begins.
It's the *Arirang* in my breast
recognizing the *Arirang* in your breast.
In the 1890s Isabella Bird Bishop, during her four visits to Joseon, recognized
that the Joseon people's sole *raison d'être*
was to provide blood to blood-sucking vampires,
and that there was *Arirang*, *Arirang* was not a noun
but a verb.
Holding out thorns to one another, rubbing, aching, pricking,
but still, since the flowing blood was warm.

That's what love is.
When the *Arirang* inside your breast

[*Arirang:* The title of the most familiar Korean song, in which a female voice expresses sorrow and bitterness because her lover has left her.]

나의 가슴 안에 있는 아리랑을 만났을 때
모든 피아노에 흰 건반과 검은 건반이 있듯
생소하지가 않아서, 혈연처럼 참회처럼
온갖 독극물과 피와 쥐약과 정액에 시체 방부제까지 섞인
더러운 한강 물속으로 뛰어들려다가
잠시 멈춰
네 가슴의 녹슨 피아노를 손으로 어루만지듯
미친 아리랑을 피아간에 아득하게 들어주는 것이다

2. 부용산

장사익의 찔레꽃이나
이애주의 부용산이나
그런 노래 듣고 있을 때
일천 개의 가을 산이 다가오다가
일천 개의 가을 산이 무너지더라도
13월의 태양처럼
세상을 한 번 산 위로 들었다 놓는 마음

노래가 뭐냐?
마음이 세상에 나오면 노래가 된다는
장사익의 말....
그래서 아리랑이 나왔지,
하얀 꽃 찔레꽃 찔러 찔려 가며
그래서 나왔지, 찔리다 못해 그만 둥그래진 아리랑이
둥그래진, 멍그래진,
찔렸지 울었지 그래 목놓아 울면서 흘러가노라

장사익의 〈찔레꽃〉이나
이애주의 〈부용산〉이나
그렇게 한번 세상을 산 위로 들었다 놓는 마음
13월의 태양 아래
찔레꽃 장미꽃 호랑가시 꽃나무가

met the Arirang inside my breast,
since they were not unfamiliar,
just as every piano has white keys and black keys
like blood ties, like repentance,
as if stroking your breast's rusty piano with a hand
after leaping into the filthy Han River
where embalming fluid mingles with all kinds of poison, blood, rat-killer,
                                                                       and semen,
then stopping briefly,
it's hearing far-off a crazy Arirang from either side.

2. BUYONG MOUNTAIN

Whenever I hear songs like
Jang Sa-Ik's 'Wild Rose'
or Lee Ae-Ju's 'Buyongsan,'
though a thousand autumn mountains draw near,
though a thousand autumn mountains collapse,
like the sun of the thirteenth month
my heart picks up the world once and sets it above the mountains.

What is a song?
Jang Sa-Ik said
that when the heart comes out into the world it turns into a song. . . .
therefore, *Arirang* emerged,
white flower, wild rose, pricking, stabbing,
therefore, it emerged, fully pricked, finally rounded, *Arirang*
rounded, bruised,
pricked till it cried, indeed, crying bitterly, it flowed away.

Either Jang Sa-Ik's 'Wild Rose'
or Lee Ae-Ju's 'Buyongsan,'
a heart like that, set the world once above the mountains
under the sun of the thirteenth month
wild rose, rose bush, holly tree,

연한 호박손이 되고 꽃순이 되고
흩어지는 민들레 홀씨로 날아갈 때까지
마음이 마구 세상에 흘러나오고 싶은 그 순간까지
숨을 참고 기다리다
하늘만 푸르러 푸르러
그런 아리랑

   3. 론도 카프리치오소

피를 팔아 산 피아노의 이야기와
피를 팔아 산 피아노가 밥이 된 이야기와
피를 팔아 산 쌀이 밥이 되었다 똥이 된 이야기와
그런 똥과 오줌이 또 내 피가 된 그런 이야기
피아노에 묻은 피, 그런 저런 이야기들이
강물 속으로 흘러들어 가고 있다

돌 속의 물고기와
빙하 속의 물고기와
청산가리 속의 물고기여
5 18 부상자 중 10%는 자살이요
자살이라네 가자 가자 흘러가자
세상에서 가장 아름다운 빛깔
델마와 루이스가 영화 마지막에 차를 몰고 투신하던
그 절벽,
그 절벽의 분홍색 흙의 빛깔, 극락의 빛깔,
그랜드 캐년도 먼 옛날엔 바다 밑에 있었다
어떻게 해서 그렇게 아름다운 빛깔을 얻었다,
그렇게 갑자기 바다 속의 피아노가
피 묻은 가슴으로 산 위에 우뚝 솟았다,

물 속의 피아노가 갑자기
산 위의 피아노가 되는 날,
갑자기 절벽의 이야기가 되는 날, 솟구쳐
돌 속의 물고기와 빙하 속의 물고기와
청산가리 속의 물고기가

turning into fine pumpkin tendrils, a bouquet of flowers,
until they go flying off as dandelion seeds,
until the moment when the heart wants to go flowing out into the world
holding its breath, waiting,
the sky alone so blue, so blue,
that *Arirang*.

3. Rondo Capriccioso

Tales of a piano that earned a living selling its blood,
tales of a piano that earned a living selling its blood becoming food,
tales of rice that earned a living selling its blood becoming food, then shit,
tales about that shit and piss becoming my blood again,
blood smeared on the piano, tales of this and that
are all flowing into the river.

Ah, the fish inside a stone and
the fish inside ice and
the fish inside potassium cyanide,
ten percent of those wounded on May 18 in Gwangju were suicides.
Suicides?
Off we go, off we go, flowing onward.
The most beautiful colour in the world.
The cliff Thelma and Louise drove off at the end of the movie,
that cliff's colour, the colour of pink earth, the colour of paradise,
and long, long ago the Grand Canyon lay under the sea.
Somehow it gained that lovely colour.
Likewise, a submarine piano suddenly
soared above the mountains, its breast smeared with blood.
The day an under-water piano
became a piano above the mountains,
the day it suddenly became a tale about a cliff, surging up,
the fish inside a stone and
the fish inside ice and
the fish inside potassium cyanide,

다 같이 함께 만세 부르며
푸르른 하늘 밑에 분홍색 극락으로 푸르러 푸르러

    4. 배고픈 승냥이의 노래

어디야, 어디야,
명사계가 어디야,
어디야, 정말, 명사계가 어디야,
누구야, 정말, 응?, 어디 가야, 어디 가야?
거울이 원죄야, 이름이 원죄야, 아니 다,
밥이 원수야, 꿈이 원수야

오늘도 그냥 일용할 고통이
쓰레기 같은 거울 산을 이루고
거울 앞에 나를 세워놓고 부려먹고 부려먹고 또 부려먹고
이 산 너머 가면 명사계 있냐고
저 산 너머 가면 명사계 있냐고
거울 뒤로 가야 명사계 나오냐고
태산 같은 땀과 태산 같은 피 흘리며
명사계가 어디냐고

어디 가야 우리 어머니 만나요?
어디 가야 내 사랑 다시 만나요?
어디 가야 해와 달 함께 만나요?

    5. 밥의 아리랑

용산이나 마포, 밥집이 많은 거리로 올라가
밥을 먹는다,
곡기를 끊고

all together crying "Manse!"
blue, blue, as a pink paradise beneath a pink sky.

4. The Song of a Hungry Coyote

Where, where,
where is Myeongsagye?
Where, truly, where is Myeongsagye?
Who? Truly, hmm? where should I go, where should I go?
Mirror is original sin. Name is original sin. Not so.
Food is the enemy. Dreams are the enemy.

Today, too, merely our daily pain,
a trash-like mirror produces mountains,
setting me before a mirror then driving me, driving me, driving me,
asking if Myeongsagye is beyond this mountain,
if Myeongsagye is beyond that mountain,
or if Myeongsagye will only emerge if I go behind the mirror,
shedding mountains of sweat, mountains of blood,
where is Myeongsagye?

Where should I go to meet Mother?
Where should I go to meet my love again?
Where should I go to meet sun and moon together?

5. Rice *Arirang*

Going up lanes with lots of eateries in Yongsan or Mapo,
I eat my food.
I give up eating.

[*Myeongsagye*: in a classic Korean novel, the world of the dead is divided into a Hell ruled over by Yama and Myeongsagye, a benevolent, maternal realm governed by the Lady Hutu where the souls of the dead are protected and enjoy rest.]

하늘도 무심하시지.... 땅을 쳐야할 상황인데도
무심하지 않으면 하늘이 아니지.... 의젓하게
혼자서 밥을 먹는다,
아리랑은 밥이다.... 아니 물에 만 밥 같은 것....
얼굴에서 얼이 다 빠지니
굴만 남았다

굴 속으로 설렁탕 국물이 막 흘러 들어간다,
생판 첨 비가 너무 많이 와
얼이 다 빠져수다....
괜히 제주 방언을 말해본다,
부담주기 싫다며
허리에 돌 24kg을 묶고
자기 집 우물 속으로 몸을 던져
빠져 죽은 어느 할머니가 있다,
첩첩 굴 속에서 정선 아리랑이
설렁탕 국물을 따라 아련히 휘돌아든다,

윤무....
뱃 속으로 휘돌아드는 노래가 있다,
얼이 다 빠져수다.... 의젓하게
얼이 빠진 굴을 들고 앉아
거울 너머 창자 속으로 흘러가는 아리랑을 바라본다,
하늘도 무심하시지....
무심하지 않으면 하늘이 아니지,
설렁탕 국물이 아련히 창자 굽이를 휘돌아든다,

그 노래가 쓰리다....

6. 흙 보다 아름다운 책은 없다

어쩌다 하늘 공원까지 왔어요,
하얗게 머리 풀고 흔들리는 망초꽃 홀씨와 억새들,
저 스스로 왔다가 저 홀로 물결처럼 흔들려요,
그 때는 사랑인 줄 모르고

Heaven doesn't care. . . . no matter how appalling a situation,
it wouldn't be Heaven if it didn't not care. . . . in a mature manner
I eat my food alone.
Arirang is food. . . . or at least something like cooked rice soaked in water. . . .
The soul has fallen away from my face,
all that's left is a hole.

Into the hole the beef soup broth goes flowing.
Too much rain has fallen,
my soul has fallen away. . . .
There once was an old woman
who did not want to be a burden
so she tied a fifty-pound stone at her waist
then threw herself into the well and died.
Inside the hole the Jeongseon *Arirang*
goes swirling round behind the beef soup broth.

circling round and round. . . .
there's a song that goes swirling into the stomach.
My soul has fallen away. . . . in a mature manner
I go into the cave it has left behind, sit down
and watch *Aririang* go flowing down into the gut.
Heaven doesn't care. . . .
it wouldn't be Heaven if it didn't not care.
The beef soup broth swirls faintly round the twists in the gut.

That song is burning.

6. THERE IS NO BOOK MORE LOVELY THAN CLAY

Somehow I've reached Sky Park.
Horsetail seeds, white hair unbound and silver grass all shaking
have come of their own accord and shake alone like waves.
At the time not realizing it was love,
squirming, bygone hours,

발버둥 치며, 지나간 시간들,
구름에 목을 걸고 살아요,
구름이 흔들리면 온몸이 나부껴요,
밥줄이란
목에서 위까지 걸려있는
그 줄이래요,
밥이 법이다
그런 말은 싫은데
몸의 한가운데, 흉곽에 피아노 철사줄이 흔들거릴 때
엘리 엘리 라마 사박다니
목구멍 속으로 울부짖는 피아노가
터져 나오려고 해요
입을 다물고 가만히 있으면
할머니도 그렇게 아팠을 거예요,
할머니도 그렇게 외로웠을 거예요,
흙이 불러요
산이 불러요
물과 바람이 불러요
막 불러요, 뿌리쳐도 불러요,
소리치며 불러요, 휘몰아치며 불러요,
흙이 그리워져요,
흙이 향기로워져요,
흙 속에 기억들이 빛나요,
할머니,
흙이 막 날아와요,
흙 묻은 억새 풀잎들이 마구 휘몰아쳐
얼굴을 덮으며 날아와요,
흙에도 날개가 뻗치는 그런 날이 있나 봐요,
그런 날
흙이 시집이예요,
흙이 전기(傳記)예요,
흙이 자서전이예요,
흙 보다 더 아름다운 책은 없는 듯해요
그러고 보니 할머니, 할머니란 말 속에 흙이 들어있네요
흙은 여인들의 아리랑이예요
할머니....

I live with a cloud about my neck.
If the cloud shakes, my whole body flutters.
My lifeline
is a line hanging from neck to stomach.
Rice is the law.
I hate those words.
When from the middle of my body the thorax's piano string sways
a piano strives to emerge
wailing *Eli Eli lama sabachthani* in my throat.
If I remain silent, clenching my teeth,
Grandmother, too, hurt just as much.
Grandmother was just as lonely.
Clay is calling.
Mountains are calling.
Water and wind are calling.
Calling loudly, calling though I shrug them off.
Shouting they call. Violently they call.
I miss the clay.
The clay grows fragrant.
Inside the clay memories glow.
Grandmother.
The clay comes flying fast.
Silver grass leaves smeared with clay rage,
come flying covering their faces.
It seems clay, too, has days when wings extend.
On such days
the clay is a book of poems.
The clay is a life story.
The clay is an autobiography.
It looks as though there is no book that is lovelier than clay.
Therefore, Grandmother, the word Grandmother contains clay.
Clay is women's *Arirang*.
Grandmother. . . .

희망이 외롭다

남들은 절망이 외롭다고 말하지만
나는 희망이 더 외로운 것 같아,
절망은 중력의 평안이라고 할까,
돼지가 삼겹살이 될 때까지
힘을 다 빼고, 그냥 피 웅덩이 속으로 가라앉으면 되는걸 뭐....
그래도 머리는 연분홍으로 웃고 있잖아, 절망엔
그런 비애의 따스함이 있네

희망은 때로 응급처치를 해주기도 하지만
희망의 응급처치를 싫어하는 인간도 때로 있을 수 있네,
아마 그럴 수 있네,
절망이 더 위안이 된다고 하면서,
바람에 흔들리는 찬란한 햇빛 한 줄기를 따라
약을 구하러 멀리서 왔는데
약이 잘 듣지 않는다는 것을 미리 믿을 정도로
당신은 이제 병이 깊었나,

희망의 토템 폴인 선인장....

사전에서 모든 단어가 다 날아가 버린 그 밤에도
나란히 신발을 벗어놓고 의자 앞에 조용히 서있는
파란 번개 같은 그 순간에도
또 희망이란 말은 간신히 남아
그 희망이란 말 때문에 다 놓아버리지도 못한다,
희망이란 말이 세계의 폐허가 완성되는 것을 가로막는다,
왜 폐허가 되도록 내버려두지 않느냐고
가슴을 두드리기도 하면서
오히려 그 희망 때문에
무섭도록 더 외로운 순간들이 있다

희망의 토템 폴인 선인장....
피가 철철 흐르도록 아직, 더, 벅차게 사랑하라는 명령인데

도망치고 싶고 그만 두고 싶어도
이유 없이 나누어주는 저 찬란한 햇빛, 아까워
물에 피가 번지듯....

HOPE IS LONELY

People often say that despair is lonely
but I reckon that hope is even lonelier.
Despair might be termed the peace of gravity.
For a pig to become bacon
all it has to do is to let go of everything and subside into a pool of blood. . . .
and still its head is grinning pink. Despair
has a similar warmth of sorrow.

Hope sometimes provides first aid
but there may sometimes be people who dislike hope's first aid,
maybe.
Reckoning that despair offers more comfort,
following a bright ray of sunlight trembling in the breeze,
I came from afar to obtain medicine
but being already convinced that the medicine has no effect
your sickness grew worse.

The cactus – hope's totem pole. . . .

Even on a night when all the words flew away from the dictionary,
even at that moment like blue lightning
standing quietly before a chair after taking off my shoes,
the word hope barely managed to remain
and because of that one word, hope, I cannot discard everything.
The word hope prevents the world's ruins from being completed.
Beating my breast
and asking why I don't let the ruins continue,
rather because of that hope
there are frighteningly lonelier times.

The cactus – hope's totem pole. . . .
it's an order to love still, more, fully, until blood flows freely

Though I want to escape, put an end to it,
that bright sunlight being shared out for no reason, such a pity,
like blood spreading in water. . . .

희망과 나,
희망은 종신형이다
희망이 외롭다

서울의 우울 6

마른 뼈 가득한 도시.
산마루마다 마른 뼈 층층이 쌓이고

누군가는 오늘 칼날 능선에서 떨어져 죽고
빙산 가운데 하늘을 향하고 누워
말 한 마디 없이 고요히 하늘을 향하고
숨을 몰아쉬고 있었다

그래 언제부터인가 산다는 것은
칼날을 부여잡고 사는 것이었지,
칼날을 잡은 쪽은 언제나 나였었다,
그러니까 그 피는 나의 피였다

칼날 능선이 있는 곳은 히말라야 낭가파르바트,
칼날 능선은 서울에 더 많이 있다,
칼날 능선에서 추락사한 사람 수도 서울이 더 많을 게다,
서울은 칼날로 이루어진
칼날능선이다

더 이상 갈 데가 없다
손이 붙잡을 것이 없다

hope and I,
hope is a life sentence.
Hope is lonely.

SEOUL MELANCHOLY 6

City full of dry bones.
Dry bones piled high on every hill.

Someone today fell from a knife-blade ridge and died,
lying amidst icebergs turned skyward
without a word, quietly turned skyward,
gasping.

True, for some time now, living
has been a matter of living clutching a knife-blade.
The one holding the knife was always me.
So that blood was my blood.

The place with the knife-blade ridge was Nanga Parbat in the Himalayas,
but there are more knife-blade ridges in Seoul.
The number of people dying after falling from knife-blade ridges is
                                          greater in Seoul, too
Seoul is a knife-blade ridge
made by a knife-blade.

There is nowhere left to go.
There is nothing for the hand to seize hold of.

서울의 우울 7

    - 메아리 기르기

메아리는 메아리가 슬펐다
메아리는 메아리, 타버린 성냥개비처럼 자기 말이 없었다
메아리는 메아리,
갔다가 오는 것,
메아리는 메아리 너머를 꿈꾸지만
메아리는 그저 갔다가 돌아올 뿐

오늘의 적이 어제의 적이 아니었으면
어제의 적은 어제의 적
오늘의 적은 오늘의 적
내일의 적은 내일의 적
전선이 그렇게 분명했으면
어제의 적이 오늘의 적이요 오늘의 적이 내일의 적이요
내일의 적이 모레의 적이고
결국 어제의 적이 모레의 적이라면

메아리는 메아리가 미웠다
메아리는 메아리, 가냘픈 메아리의 피는 파랗기만 했다
메아리는 메아리,
흘러가지 못하는 것,
무지개는 무지개, 그 너머를 꿈꾸지만
메아리는 메아리, 갔다가 오다가
파아랗게 다만 사그라지는 것,
메아리는 불현듯 울창한 피가 부러웠다

적도 사랑도, 미움도 아픔도, 죄악도 심판도,
계산도 전선도 다 안고, 뭉뚱그려 껴안고, 활활,
세상에서 가장 아름다운 꽃,
붉은 인주(印朱) 찍어 지문으로 남긴
송알송알 피 배인,
장자연의 유서
자본주의의 드라이아이스 속에 빠져 허덕이다가
끝내 빠알간 한 송이 꽃으로 꺾여
불같이 퍼덕였다, 그녀,
표표, 북망, 훨훨

SEOUL MELANCHOLY 7
   – Raising echoes

Echo as echo was sad.
Echo as echo, like a burnt-out matchstick, didn't have its own words.
Echo as echo,
what goes then comes back,
echo dreams of what lies beyond echo
but echo merely goes then comes back.

If only today's foe were not yesterday's foe,
yesterday's foe as yesterday's foe,
today's foe as today's foe,
tomorrow's foe as tomorrow's foe,
if only the line were that clear,
if yesterday's foe were today's foe, today's foe tomorrow's foe,
tomorrow's foe the following day's foe
then if yesterday's foe were the day after tomorrow's foe

Echo hated echo.
Echo as echo, the faint echo's blood was just red.
Echo as echo,
what cannot go flowing off,
rainbow as rainbow, dreams of what lies beyond but
echo as echo, going then coming,
something simply subsiding red,
echo was suddenly jealous of thick blood.

Foe and love, hatred and pain, sin and judgement,
calculation and battle-front, all embraced, lumped together
                                    and embraced, flaming,
the loveliest flower in the world,
pressed on a red ink-pad, leaving a fingerprint,
blood pearling, blood soaked
Jang Ja-Yeon's will,
after falling into capitalism's dry ice and struggling,
finally plucked as a single blossom,
fluttering like flames, that woman,
floating, another world, flaming.

서울의 우울 8
- 다리 위에 전화기

물이 목까지 차올라
자살하러 한강 다리에 갔더니 전화기가 있더라네,
물이 목까지 차올랐는데
무슨 말이 더 필요하겠는가,

이제 아무 원망도 하고 싶지 않네,
구멍으로 사라진 상상의 토끼를 구하고 싶지도 않네,
그래도 전화기를 보니
옛날 노란 전화번호부, 그 많던 이름들이 떠오르고
나에게도 전성기가 있었지.... 때 아닌 미소도 떠오르고

물이 목까지 차올랐는데
무슨 이름들이 더 필요하겠는가,
나의 수준이 너를 결정했으니
아무 얼굴도 떠오르지 않고
개도 웃고 소도 웃는 이 난망,
아열대 흡혈 거머리처럼 나를 흡입하던 귀먹은 캄캄함이여,

나의 수준이 너를 결정하였고
너의 수준이 나를 결정하였으니
자살하러 다리까지 와서 새삼 뭉크의 심연을
그려보긴 그려보더라도

물이 목까지 차올라
자살하러 한강 다리에 갔더니 전화기가 있더라네,
아무 생각도 안나는데
구멍 속으로 깡충 튀어 들어간
여보세요....상상의 토끼를 손이 마구 부르더라네

SEOUL MELANCHOLY 8
– Phone on a bridge

With water up to my chin
I went out to the Han River bridge to kill myself and there's a phone.
The water was up to my chin,
what words more did I need?

I don't want to do any more blaming now.
And I don't want to look for the imaginary rabbit that vanished down a hole.
Still, at the sight of the phone,
the old yellow directories with all those names come to mind,
I too had my salad days. . . . an untimely smile arises,

The water was up to my chin,
what names more did I need?
My standard determined you
so no face came to mind,
this unforgettable thing, a dog laughing, a cow laughing,
like the blood-sucking leeches of tropical regions,
you deaf darkness that once sucked me in.

My standard determined you
and your standard determined me
so I came out to the Han River bridge to kill myself
and even though I paint Munch's abyss
with water up to my chin,
I went out to the Han River bridge to kill myself and there's a phone.
No thought comes to me
though, Hello. . . . my hand madly calls after the imaginary rabbit
that hopped into the hole

서울의 우울 9

    - 앵무새 기르기

영혼 없는 새
남의 말을 따라 하는 새
고장난 녹음기 보다 더 나쁜 새
내 영혼을 들킬까봐 남의 말 뒤로 숨는 새
세상은 그런 새를 기르기를 원한다
그런 새를 만들려고
학교를 만들었고 입시를 만들었고
사법고시를, 언론고시를 만들었다
앵무새를 길러 놓으니 참 편해, 내 말을 다 해주잖아. . . .
한번도 아니고 두 번도 아니고 매번 그렇게. . . .
참 고마워라,
숲에서 우는 소쩍새여, 꾀꼬리여, 부엉이여,
놀라워라
제 소리로 제 슬픔을 애통하며
에레미아 선지자처럼
세세년년
남의 슬픔을 관통하는 새
앵무새는 죽어도 못 따라 갈
영혼 고운
새

서울의 우울 10

    - 장자연의 꽃송이

꽃이다
꽃송이다
핏빛 지장(指章) 찍어
꽃송이를 남겼다
유서를 쓰려거든 똑 이렇게 쓰렸다!
원수여, 내가 너를 단죄하러 가는 길,
원수의 이름도 모르고

SEOUL MELANCHOLY 9

    – Raising a parrot

A bird with no soul.
A bird that repeats people's words.
A bird worse that a broken recording machine.
A bird hiding behind people's words lest it find out my soul.
The world wants to raise such a bird.
Intent on manufacturing such a bird
it established a school, established an entrance exam,
established a bar exam, a press exam.
Having raised a parrot, it's very convenient, it says all my words. . . .
Not just once, not just twice, but all the time. . . .
I am really grateful.
You birds singing in the woods, Scops owl, oriole, owl,
wonderful,
you lament your sorrows in your own voices
like Jeremiah the Prophet,
for ever and ever,
birds that penetrate people's sorrows,
each being a bird
with a beautiful soul,
that a parrot can never hope to emulate.

SEOUL MELANCHOLY 10

    – Jang Ja-Yeon's flower

It's a flower.
It's a single blossom.
Having printed a blood-red thumb-print
she left behind a blossom.
Intending to write a final message, that was all she wrote.
My enemy, on my way to punish you,
ignorant of your name,

원수의 집도 모르고
원수의 눈 코 입 면상도 모른 채
원수여, 사는 자와 파는 자, 먹는 자와 먹히는 자,
매매된 자와 매매한 자 사이에 원수가 성립이 될까?
어쨌든, 서울이 소비한 여자, 나 보다 빠르고
언제나 나보다 고상하고
언제나 나보다 힘센....
너는 여기에도 있고
거기에도 있고
너는 여기에도 없고 거기에도 없고
나의 말을 나보다 더 많이 갖고 있고
나의 눈동자를 솔개보다 더 빨리 파먹고
악수를 하며 복수를 하고 복수를 하며 악수를 하는
원수여,
원수는 언제나 벅차다
너를 찾아 단도를 품고 가는 길
집도 모르고 코도 몰라

하얀, 흰, 허어연
광목에 동백처럼, 광목에 양귀비, 광목에 목단처럼
붉은 지장을 찍고
꽃송이 몇 송이 목숨 다해 친필로 흩뿌렸나니
유서를 쓰려면 똑 이렇게 쓰렸다!
유서 한 장 남기고
오늘도 원수를 찾아 오월 만발 초록 길을 걷나니
찢어진 옷고름
피 묻은 흰 치마
그러면 그럴수록 하늘만 푸르고
그러면 그럴수록 깨끗이 면도한
아침 서울의 면상

ignorant of your home,
ignorant of your eyes, nose, mouth, face,
my enemy, between buyer and seller, eater and eaten,
seller and sold, shall we establish enmity?
In any case, the woman consumed by Seoul, faster than me,
ever more sophisticated than me,
ever stronger than me. . . .
you are here
and you are there,
you are not here, not there,
you have more of my words than I have,
you peck out my eyes quicker than a hawk,
shaking my hand you take revenge, taking revenge you shake my hand,
my enemy,
you are always full to the brim.
On my way, seeking you, clutching a dagger,
knowing neither house nor nose.

White, whitish, off-white,
like camellias on cotton, like poppies, like peonies on cotton,
signed with a red thumbprint,
a few flowers, once life is over, scattered in handwriting,
if you mean to write a will, this is how to write it!
As today again I walk along the green road in full bloom, seeking my enemy,
leaving a will behind,
a torn breast-tie,
a white skirt stained with blood,
more and more the sky alone is blue,
more and more clean-shaven,
Seoul's early-morning face.

from
A CROAKER ON A CHOPPING BOARD

꽃들의 제사

어떤 그리움이 저 달리아 같은 붉은 꽃물결을 피게 하는가
어떤 그리움이 혈관 속에 저 푸른 파도를 울게 하는가
어떤 그리움이 저 흰 구름을 밀고 가는가
어떤 그리움이 흘러가는 강물 위에 저 반짝이는 햇빛을 펄떡이게 하는가
어떤 그리움이 끊어진 손톱과 끊어진 손톱을 이어놓는가
어떤 그리움이 저 돌멩이에게 중력을 잊고 뜨게 하는가
어떤 그리움이 시카다(cicada)에게 17년 동안의 지하 생활을 허하는가
어떤 그리움이 시카다에게 한여름 대낮의 절명가를 허하는가
어떤 그리움이 저 비행운과 비행운을 맺어주나
지금 파란 하늘을 보는 이 심장은 뛰고 있다
불타는 심장은 꽃들의 제사다
이 심장에는 지금 유황의 온천수 같은
뜨거운 김이 모락모락 피어오르고 있는데

맨드라미의 시간에

꽃이 도마에 오른다
말도 안 되는 희망이라니
그런 말도 안 되는 꽃이 도마 위에 놓였다,
계절 따라 피는 꽃들도 도마 위에 오르면
오스스 소름이 오른다, 소름이 돋아 피가 뭉쳐
도마 위에서 꽃은 붉은 볏으로 솟아난다,
얼굴이 빡빡 얽은 붉은 얼금뱅이가
고장난 시계를 안고 도마 위 꽃밭에 만발한다,
도마 위에선 내일이 없기 때문에
두 눈 뜨고도 앞을 못 보기 때문에
내일이란 말을 모르는 맨드라미 얼굴에 붉고 서러운 이빨이 돋아난다
터널 끝에도 빛이 보이지 않을 때
우리는 그것을 맨드라미의 시간이라 부른다

FLOWERS' MEMORIAL RITES

What yearning can be making that sea of dahlia-like flowers bloom red?
What yearning can be making that blue wave weep in my veins?
What yearning is pushing that cloud?
What yearning can be making the sunlight flutter as it sparkles on that
flowing stream?
What yearning links severed fingernail with severed fingernail?
What yearning can be making that pebble forget gravity and float?
What yearning enables a cicada to spend 17 years underground?
What yearning brings together that vapour trail and this vapour trail?
The heart now looking at that blue sky is racing.
A blazing heart is the flowers' memorial rites.
Now hot steam like that from a sulphuric hot spring
is billowing up in this heart of mine.

COCKSCOMB TIME

Flowers clamber up onto the chopping board.
Hope being preposterous,
similarly preposterous flowers take their place on the chopping board.
When flowers that blossom according to the season mount the chopping board
they develop gooseflesh; as the gooseflesh erupts the blood clots
and on the chopping board the flowers erupt as red crests,
their faces pockmarked red embracing broken clocks,
blossom in flower beds on the chopping board,
and because on the chopping board there is no tomorrow,
because they are blind even with eyes open,
in the cockscomb faces that know nothing of the word tomorrow sad,
red teeth emerge.
When there is no light to be seen at the end of the tunnel
we call that cockscomb time.

피안을 거슬러
화단의 모든 꽃들과 돌들이 혹서를 치르고 있는 어느 여름날
바위마저도 스스로 다비하는 듯
우리는 그런 시간을 뜨겁고 붉은
맨드라미의 마그나 카르타라고 불러야 한다
해를 바라보며 목마름으로 더 타오르다 서서 죽는다

오른편 심장 하나 주세요

사랑은 머리 위로 떨어지는 칼
손으로 잡으면 늘 다치는 것
사랑은 가슴 위로 떨어지는 피
피하려고 해도 꼭 적시는 것

세상은 온통 배롱나무 꽃 천지
지금은 꽃의 피가
사방 공기에 다 물들었다

앞으로 갈 길에는 주유소가 없을 것 같다는 느낌
기름이 거의 떨어져 가는데
다음 주유소는 나오지 않을 것 같다는 느낌

여기서부터다
주유소가 안 나오면
꽃의 피로 가야지,
못 박힌 자리에서 쏟아지는 피,
오른편 심장 하나 구하려고 배롱나무 꽃그늘에

One summer's day when all the flowers in the garden and even the stones
suffer from heat, defying enlightenment,
as if even the rocks are being cremated,
we should call that time a scorching red
cockscomb's Magna Carta.
Dying erect, gazing up at the sun, blazing with thirst.

GIVE ME A HEART ON THE RIGHT-HAND SIDE

Love's a sword dropping onto your head;
if you try to grab it, you're sure to be wounded.
Love's blood dropping onto the breast –
though you try to avoid it, you're sure to be soaked.

The world's all made up of crape myrtle flowers
and now those flower's blood
has dyed the air in all directions.

The feeling that there's no filling station along the road ahead;
the feeling that you're nearly out of fuel
and there's no sign of a filling station ahead.

From here on,
if no filling station appears,
I'll have to run on the blood of flowers,
the blood pouring from the place the nails were driven in,
intent on obtaining a heart on the right-hand side
in the shadow of crepe myrtle flowers.

해바라기와 꿀벌

해바라기 꽃잎 속에 고개를 파묻고
꿀벌은 성경을 읽듯이 꿀에 집중하고 있었다,
그 집중에는 이상하게도 서러움과 성스러움이 있었다,
누우면 발끝이 벽에 닿는 창문 없는 쪽방에서
서로의 몸 밖에는 구할 것이 아무것도 없는 젊은 가난
우주의 한 구석지에서 쟁, 쟁, 쟁, 타오르는 해바라기 몸
종소리마다 박히는 크고 검은 씨앗, 탐스런 꿀에 고개를 박고
차라리 모든 괴롬을 던져버린 날들도 있었을 것이다,
미래라는 단어만한 사치도 없었을 것이다,
죽어도 좋아,
가난한 꿀벌의 등은 등 뒤에 걸린 칼날을 찰나찰나 예감하고
파르르 떨리기도 했을 것이다,
꿀에 머리를 박고 고요히 등 뒤의 칼날을 느끼며
꿀 송이에 빠져 있는 깊은 꿀벌의 모습이
아프도록 슬픈 성자의 사색 어린 모습과 어딘지 닮아 있던 것이다

칼갈이 광고 차

강변북로, 출근길에,
추월 차선을 가로막고
'무료 출장 방문 칼갈이' 광고를 붙인 봉고차가 간다
급한 일이 없는가
추월 차선을 가로막고 세월아 네월아 느릿느릿 간다

'칼의 부활 가위도 부활'
'방문 칼갈이, 직접 방문하여 칼을 갈아드립니다'
검은 바탕에 선정적인 빨간 페인트 광고 글자,
봉고차는 보란듯이 계속 내 앞을 막고 천천히 간다
집에 있는 무뎌진 칼들이 생각나고

SUNFLOWER AND HONEYBEE

Its head buried among sunflower petals,
the honeybee was absorbed in honey as if reading the Bible,
and strangely enough in that absorption there was sorrow and sanctity,
in the windowless cell where feet touched the wall when lying down,
poor kids with nothing apart from one another's bodies,
a sunflower body blazing in one corner of the universe,
large black seeds driven in by every peal of the bell,
its head plunged into appetizing honey,
there must have been days when every care was cast aside,
there must have been no luxury equal to the word future,
longing to die,
the honeybee must have sensed briefly the blade hanging behind its back
and trembled, *brrr.*
Its head plunged into honey, quietly feeling the blade behind its back,
the sight of the honeybee plunged deep into honey-blossom
somehow resembled
the sight of a saint plunged in meditation, so sad that it hurt.

THE KNIFE GRINDER'S ADVERTISING CAR

On the Gangbyeon Expressway on my way to work,
blocking the overtaking lane,
a van goes trundling along displaying signs:
"Knife-grinding, free home visits."
Obviously there's no emergency,
at a snail's pace, taking its time, trundling on.

"Knives reborn, scissors reborn."
"Knives ground at home. We visit and grind."
Suggestive ads written in red paint on a black ground.
The van continues to drive along slowly, proudly blocking my way.
I think of the blunt knives I have at home:

부엌칼, 쌍둥이 칼, 회칼, 과도, 고기 칼,
칼을 갈았던 게 언제인지 온갖 살림살이마다 엉망인데

살려고 하면 죽은 체하라, 죽은 체하면 삶이 온단다. . . .
맥베스 마녀들의 돌림노래소리
칼을 품고 사는 마음은 버리고 싶었는데
"무뎌졌다" 그 말 한마디를 던지고
투신자살했던 부산대 교수가 생각나고
칼도 예술이다, 그런 말도 생각나는데
발을 동동 그르는 숨가쁜 출근길에
좀 비켜줘라! 강의에 늦는다고요!
강의에 늦는 것은 아무것도 아니라고
칼갈이 광고 차는 천천히
추월 차선을 가로막고 세월아 네월아 내 앞을 가고 있다
보이지도, 보이지도 않는 향기로운 칼이

작년의 달력

12장의 그림 달력을 다 넘겼을 때
그 순간
속수무책이다
손써볼 도리가 없다
지구를 들어올리고 있던 힘줄이 일시에 다 끊어졌다

마지막 달력엔 이방의 성당 그림이 있었다
성당 안에는 가느다란 촛불들이 자작자작 타오르고 있었다
촛불 하나에 천사 하나씩
흰 뼈가 다 드러난 양초의 향기와 반짝임이 가득했다
그 많은 촛불은 무슨 기도를 올리고 있었을까

kitchen knives, twin knives, fillet knives, fruit knives, carving knives,
no idea when they last were sharpened, housekeeping's all a mess.

If you would live, pretend to be dead; if you pretend to be dead, life comes.
The song of Macbeth's witches.
I recall that Busan University professor who,
longing to rid himself of a life with a heart clutching a hidden knife,
drowned himself after shouting a single phrase: "I've lost my edge."
Knives, too, are art. I recall that saying, too.
Breathlessly stamping on my way to work,
"Out of my way! I'll be late for class!"
"Being late for class is nothing,"
the knife grinder's advertising car slowly goes trundling on
at a snail's pace, taking its time,
blocking the overtaking lane ahead of me.
Seen or unseen, fragrant knives.

LAST YEAR'S CALENDAR

Reaching the end of an illustrated calendar's twelve pages,
is a moment
of utter helplessness.
There is nothing I can do.
The sinew that had been holding up the Earth suddenly snapped.

On the last page was the picture of a foreign church.
Inside the church slender candle flames were burning.
Each flame was an angel
full of the perfume and sparkle of the bony candle.
I wonder what prayers all those candle flames were offering up?

단 한 개의 숫자만으로도 가슴을 깨뜨릴 수가 있는 곳
속수무책인 곳
지상의 모든 악기의 줄이 일시에 다 끊어지고
심장을 포함한 모든 악기 소리가 금지된 한순간
화들짝 가슴을 깨뜨리는
작년의 달력

인간의 눈물이 있었고
아름다운 호소로 가득찬 호수가 있었고
다친 손이 있었고
그림 속에 날개 달린 천사도 있었다

한겨울 밤의 서정시

무섭게 추운 캄캄한 밤
가게들은 다 셔터 문을 내렸다
새도 별도 나뭇가지도 빙하 속에 갇혀 화석이 된 듯
거리엔 아무 기척이 없다
폐렴 걸린 패랭이꽃 같은 파르스름한 하현의 달
달의 눈썹에도 하얀 얼음이 끼었다
그리움도 기다림도 갈 길을 잃었다
불 꺼진 거리 모퉁이에
원룸촌이 있고
그 옆에 작은 코인 세탁소가 있다
불이 환하다
코인 세탁소 유리창엔 성에의 무늬가 반짝거리고 있다
세제의 향기가 살풋 끼쳐오고
빨래 삶는 하얀 수증기가 풍풍 올라가고 있다
따뜻한 비누 거품 속에
돌아가는 세탁통 안에는
색색의 티셔츠랑 브래지어랑 팬티랑 양말이 돌아가고 있다
와이셔츠랑 바지랑 란제리도 자기들끼리 돌아가고 있다

A place where the heart can be broken by just a single date,
a place of utter helplessness,
a moment when the strings of all the world's musical instruments snapped
and the sound of every instrument that contained a heart was prohibited.
In last year's calendar,
abruptly heart-breaking,

were people's tears,
a lake full of beautiful appeals,
wounded hands,
angels with wings like in a picture.

A MIDWINTER NIGHT'S LYRIC POEM

A dreadful cold, dark night,
all the shops had lowered their shutters,
birds and stars and branches, enclosed in ice, all seemed turned into fossils,
there was no sign of anyone in the streets.
The blue moon in its final quarter hung like a carnation stricken with pneumonia,
and the moon's eyebrows were painted thick with white frost.
Yearning and waiting had lost their way.
At the unlit corner of the street
was a block of one-room studios
and beside that was a small laundromat,
brightly lit.
On the laundromat's windows patterns of frost were glistening.
The smell of detergent came gently drifting
while the steam from the laundry being washed was rising white.
In the warm soapy foam
inside the spinning drums
multicoloured T-shirts, brassieres, panties, socks were turning.
Shirts, shorts, lingerie were turning, each in separate batches.

아무도 없는 캄캄한 한밤중에
쏟아지는 세탁 물방울 하나하나 속에 설핏 무지개가 비치고
여러해살이풀처럼 스러졌다 다시 서는
어제의 빨래들

무서운 밤이 흰 떡국처럼 참 따뜻하다

전망

신의 절개지가 눈앞에 펼쳐져 있다
바로 눈앞은 아니고 저기 저 앞이다
그러니까 나의 전망은 신의 절개지다
생살이 찢어진 붉은 절개지에도 사계절이 오고
나무뿌리가 지하수를 끌어올리고
새순이 돋아나고 꽃도 피고 열매도 열린다
절개지는 절개의 상처를 치료하려고 사계절 내내
저렇게 노력하고 있다
태초에 그리움은 그렇게 만들어진 것이다
다음에 무엇이 올지 모르면서
저만치
절개지 너머의 반쪽 산은 절개지 너머의 이쪽 산을 바라본다
장마철이면 또 생살이 찢어지던
절개지의 아픔이 시뻘겋게 되살아나 흙탕을 치고 내려온다
지금도 펄펄 살아 있는 저 붉은 아픔은
절개지의 절벽 위에 피어난
한 움큼의 야생화로 스스로 치료하려는 듯
갈 봄 여름 없이 조촐한 꽃들이 피었다 진다

On that dark winter's night with nobody in sight
in each gushing water-drop from the washing machines a rainbow
                                                            gleamed softly,
yesterday's laundry
fell and rose again like perennial plants.

The dreadful night felt really warm, like white rice-cake soup

PROSPECT

God's landslip is spread out before my eyes.
Not right before my eyes but over there.
So my prospect is God's landslip.
In that red landslip rending living flesh the four seasons come,
tree roots draw up water from underground,
buds emerge, flowers bloom, fruits form.
The landslip tries hard throughout the four seasons
to heal the wound of the incision.
In the beginning that's how yearning is made.
Ignorant of what may follow,
over there
half the hill beyond the landslip is contemplating the hill on this side.
When the rains come, the pain of the landslip
that rent living flesh again revives scarlet,
forms a muddy flood pouring down a waterway.
Still now, that living, vivid red pain,
as if intent on healing itself with a handful of wild flowers
blooming above the landslip's precipice,
while regardless of seasons simple flowers blossom and wither.

좌파/우파/허파

시곗바늘은 12시부터 6시까지는 우파로 돌다가
6시부터 12시까지는 좌파로 돈다
미친 사람 빼고
시계가 좌파라고, 우파라고 말하는 사람은 없다
아무리 바빠도 벽에 걸린 시계 한번 보고 나서 말해라

세수는 두 손바닥으로 우편향 한 번 좌편향 한 번
그렇게
이루어진다
그렇게 해야 낯바닥을 온전히 닦을 수 있는 것이다

시곗바늘도 세수도 구두도 스트레칭도
좌우로 왔다갔다하면서 세상은 돌아간다
필히 구두의 한쪽은 좌파이고 또다른 쪽은 우파이다
그렇게 좌우는 홀로 가는 게 아니다
게다가 지구는 돈다

좌와 우의 사이에는
청초하고도 서늘한, 다사롭고도 풍성한
평형수가 흐르는 정원이 있다
에덴의 동쪽도 에덴의 서쪽도
다 숨은 샘이 흐르는 인간의 땅
허파도 그곳에서 살아 숨쉰다

LEFT / RIGHT / LUNGS

From 12 until 6 the hands of a clock turn on the right.
From 6 until 12 they turn on the left.
Except for crazy guys
nobody says the clock is right-wing or left-wing.
No matter how busy, just look at the clock on the wall once and tell me so.

Face-washing, too, is done
by the two palms,
one on the right, one on the left.
It's the only way to fully cleanse the whole face.

Clock hands, face-washing, shoes and stretching, too,
all move to and fro between left and right and so the world goes round.
Necessarily one shoe will be for the left, the other for the right.
Neither left nor right move on alone.
And so the world rotates.

In-between left and right
there's a garden, elegant and cool, warm and abundant
where weighty water flows.
East of Eden, West of Eden,
both are humanity's land where hidden springs flow.
That's where our lungs live and breathe.

'알로하'라는 말

그냥 알로하 한마디면 된단다
모든 좋은 것은 알로하로 통한단다

심장, 이 부드러운 향기의 힘
난초 꽃을 피우며 밀고 올라가는 힘
바다와 하늘이 서로를 비추는 이 유유한 힘
산마루와 골짜기가 서로 사랑하는 이 애절한 힘

오늘은 마음이 구름과 자유를 추구한단다
사랑이나 희망이나
그렇게 너무 어려운 불치병은 모래밭 속에 묻고
기세등등하지 마

알로하,
한마디면 된단다
희망에는 완치가 없지만
절망에는 완치가 있다고

구름같이 유유한 신의 자애로움을 따라
미소 한 포기를 가슴에 꽂고
한 걸음씩 한 걸음씩 조용히 가세요,
꽃피는 시절에 다시 만나리,
그냥 알로하 한마디면 된단다

노숙의 일가친척

해골의 윤곽이 그려진 초안에
밤이 내리면
꽃들도 꽃잎을 접고 노숙할 준비를 하고
나무들도 날개를 접고 노숙을 하고
새들도
묘지도 노숙을 하고

THE WORD 'ALOHA'

That one word "Aloha" all alone is enough, it seems.
Everything good is expressed by "Aloha".

The heart, the power of its gentle fragrance,
the power pushing up an orchid as it blooms,
the leisurely power with which sea and sky illuminate each other,
the mournful power of mountain ridge and valley loving one another.

Today, the heart seeks clouds and freedom, it seems.
Do not put on a bold front
and bury in a sandbank over-difficult incurable diseases,
such as love or hope.

"Aloha",
that one word is enough, it seems.
There is no full recovery from hope but
there is a complete recovery from despair, it seems.

Following God's leisurely, cloudlike tenderness,
pinning a smile onto the breast,
let's advance one step after another.
We will meet again when flowers bloom,
so the one word "Aloha" is enough, it seems.

ONE FAMILY SLEEPING OUT

When night falls
over the draft of a drawing of a skull's outline,
flowers fold their petals and prepare to sleep out in the open,
trees fold their wings and sleep outside,
birds, too,
and graveyards sleep in the open air.

달도 노숙을 하고
강과 하늘이 서로 거울이 되는 양
별들도 강물 안에 노숙을 하러 멀리서 내려온다
아름다운 것들은 다 노숙을 하고 있다
무한한 것들은 다 노숙을 한다

노숙을 하는 묘지의 별 위로
노숙을 하는 새들이 잠시 새벽을 스치고
이슬이 몸을 털고 일어나는 아침
질경이 달개비 민들레 들아
너희들도 함께 노숙을 했구나
무비자 속에 비자가 있고
무조건 속에 조건이 있고
무연고 속에 연고가 있듯이
노숙이 노숙을 위로하는구나

노숙의 일가친척들을 거느리고
오늘밤이 또 묘지 곁으로 무한 속으로 나온다

우체국과 헌 구두

환한 햇살 아래 우체국 가는 길
발목에서 흘러내리는 검정 스타킹 같은 그림자가 길다
수취인의 이름과 주소를 소중하게 가슴에 품고
우체국에는 목마른 사람들이 붐빈다
우체국에는 선인장에 물을 주는 손이 있다
멀리 있는 딸의 주소를 적고
품목 칸에 헌 구두 두 켤레라고 적고 선물이라고 적고
그다음 가치를 적어야 한다
난해한 질문은 이것이다
가치는 곧 가격을 말한단다

The moon, too, sleeps outside
and while river and sky serve as one another's mirror
the stars come down from afar to sleep out in the river.
Beautiful things all sleep outside.
Boundless things all sleep out.

In the morning, above the cemetery's stars sleeping outside,
birds sleeping out briefly brush past the dawn,
dewdrops brush themselves off and rise.
Why, plantain, spiderwort, dandelion,
you too slept out with them!

Just as there are visas inside "visa-free,"
conditions inside "unconditional,"
family and friends inside "without family or friends,"
so one "sleeping outside" comforts the other "sleeping outside."

Taking care of "sleeping outside's" kith and kin,
tonight emerges in the limitless spaces beside the graveyard.

THE POST OFFICE AND OLD SHOES

On my way to the post office in bright sunshine
the shadows flowing from my ankles like black stockings are long.
I hold the recipient's name and address carefully to my breast.
The post office is thronged with thirsty people.
The post office has someone watering the cactus.
After writing down the address of my far-away daughter,
I write "two pairs of used shoes" in the item-description box, then "gift".
Next I have to write down the value.
Now that's a tricky question.
Value, it seems, means the price.

가격이 곧 가치는 아닌데
딸의 헌 구두 두 켤레를 싣고 비행기는 하늘로 날아간다
금 없는 하늘에서 비행기는 아름답기만 하다
마음은 특급 국제 소포의 배송 경로를 따라간다
산을 넘고 바다를 건너 소포는 간다
하늘의 심장을 지나 구름의 심장도 통과한다
갈 곳을 찾아서 꼭 갈 곳으로 간다
그리고 지상에는 우체국이 있다
국경없는의사회처럼 우체국도 그렇다
그리움은 누룩을 품고 날아가는데
지상에서의 귀중한 가치로 우체국을 꼭 믿는 마음이 있다
가격이 문제가 아니라 가치가 문제라면
우체국이 무너진다면
인간의 체온도 사계절도 모든 가치에도 금이 갈 것만 같다

'이미'라는 말 2

이미라는 말
하나의 세계에 고요히 문을 닫는 말
이미라는 말 뒤에는 아무것도 없다는 말,
미래가 미래를 완료하는 말,
누구도 누구를 구원할 수 없는 시간의 말,
문상객도 없이 병풍만 쳐놓은 그런 말,
박제가 박제를 완료하는 말,

이미라는 말에는
핏기 잃은 지상의 마지막 기도뿐
이미라는 말에는
바깥에서 아무것도 들어올 수 없는
'이미'라는 미래완료의 시간과
지금은 단지 어두운 그 통로를 천천히 걸어가는 소슬한 시간

The price is not necessarily the value.
The plane flies up into the sky carrying two pairs of my daughter's old shoes.
In the unfissured sky the plane is simply beautiful.
The heart follows the delivery route of the international express parcel.
Over the mountains, across the sea, the parcel goes.
It passes through the heart of the sky and the heart of the clouds.
It will find out where it has to go and go there.

And on earth there is a post office.
The post office is just like Doctors Without Borders.
As longing goes flying off embracing leaven,
there is a heart that trusts the post office as a precious value on earth.
If the value matters more than the price,
if the post office collapses,
it seems that human body heat and the four seasons, too, will simply crack.

THE WORD 'ALREADY' 2

The word "already"
is a word that quietly shuts the door on a world,
a word saying that behind the word already there is nothing,
a word for the future completing the future,
a word for the time when nobody can save someone,
such a word as erects a funeral screen though there are no mourners,
a word for stuffed animals completing stuffed animals.

In the word "already"
is nothing but the earth's last prayer that has lost its colour,
in the word "already"
is the future perfect time known as "already"
into which nothing can enter from outside,
and desolate time now slowly goes walking along that merely dark road.

알로하 꽃목걸이

호놀룰루, 화산섬이다

삶을 한번 망친 사람들을 위해서
호놀룰루 하늘은 그렇게 온화한 파란색으로 떠 있다

여기서 저 파란 하늘은 시신을 덮어주는 수의나
신생아의 미사포 너울
간호사의 옷깃이기도 하다

릴리우오칼라니
패망한 왕조의 마지막 여왕
알로하 꽃다발을 만드는 난초 꽃처럼 향기로운
슬픔

그녀의 손이 향기를 꿰어 꽃목걸이를 만든다
알로하 향기는
한번 자기 생을 망친 사람들의 아픈 몸을 바라보며
손을 잡고 맥을 짚어준다

여행으로의 초대

모르는 곳으로 가서
모르는 사람이 되는 것이 좋다,
모르는 도시에 가서
모르는 강 앞에서
모르는 언어를 말하는 사람들과 나란히 앉아
모르는 오리와 더불어 일광욕을 하는 것이 좋다
모르는 새들이 하늘을 날아다니고
여기가 허드슨 강이지요
아는 언어를 잊어버리고
언어도 생각도 단순해지는 것이 좋다
모르는 광장 옆의 모르는 작은 가게들이 좋고

ALOHA, LEIS OF WELCOME

Honolulu is a volcanic island.

Honolulu's sky floats serene and blue
for people who have screwed up their lives.

Here, that blue sky serves as the shroud covering a corpse,
or a new-born baby's veil,
a nurse's collar.

Liliuokalani
was the last ruler of a fallen dynasty,
her sorrow
was fragrant like the flowers forming a lei of welcome.

Her hands string fragrances to make leis.
The fragrance of aloha
beholds the sick bodies of those who have screwed up their lives,
grasps their hands, feels their pulse.

INVITATION TO A JOURNEY

Going to an unknown place
and becoming an unknown person is good.
Going to an unknown city,
sitting beside people speaking an unknown language
beside an unknown river
and sunbathing with unknown ducks is good.
Unknown birds fly across the sky –
surely this is the Hudson River?
Forgetting the languages you know,
language and thoughts growing simpler, is good.
The unknown little stores beside an unknown plaza are good.

모르는 거리 모퉁이에서 모르는 파란 음료를 마시고
모르는 책방에 들어가 모르는 책 구경을 하고
모르는 버스 정류장에서 모르는 주소를 향하는
각기 피부색이 다른 모르는 사람들과 서서
모르는 버스를 기다리며
너는 그들을 모르고 그들도 너를 모르는
자유가 좋고
그 자유가 너무 좋고 좋은 것은
네가 허드슨 강을 흐르는
한 포기 모르는 구름 이상의 것이 아니라는
그것이 좋기 때문이다
그것이 좋고
모르는 햇빛 아래 치솟는 모르는 분수의 노래가 좋고
모르는 아이들의 모르는 웃음소리가 좋고
모르는 세상의 모르는 구름이 많이 들어올수록
모르는 나의 미지가 넓어지는 것도 좋아
나는 나도 모르게 비를 맞고 좀 나은 사람이 될 수도 있겠지
모르는 새야 모르는 노래를 많이 불러다오
모르는 내일을 모르는 사랑으로 가벼이 받으련다

트로이의 시간

트로이에서
허드슨 강변에서
햇빛이 섞인 바닥분수의 물을 맞으며 노는 아이들,
태어난 것이 선물이고 하루하루가 축복
이런 말을 하며 놀고 있는가,
하루는 이렇게 흘러가고
다시 만날 수 없는 사람들이
해바라기 복판 같은 시계 속에서 춤추고 있는데
이 순간의 행복
이것 외에 다른 것이 없다면

Drinking an unknown green drink on an unknown street corner,
going into an unknown bookstore and looking at unknown books,
then standing with unknown people, each with differently-coloured skin,
on their way to unknown addresses
waiting for an unknown bus,
the freedom of you not knowing them, they not knowing you, is good
and what is good about the way that freedom is good
is because you are no more than a scrap of unknown cloud
with the Hudson River flowing, and that is good.
That is good
and the song of an unknown fountain playing in unknown sunlight is good,
the unknown laughter of unknown children is good,
and the way my unknown ignorance expands,
as the more the unknown clouds of an unknown world come drifting is good,
so I can be soaked in unknown rain without knowing it
and so become a better person, surely.
You unknown bird, sing an unknown song, I beg.
I long to lightly welcome an unknown tomorrow with an unknown love.

TROY TIME

In Troy,
beside the Hudson River, maybe the kids
playing in ground fountains' water mingled with sunlight
are saying as they play: being born is a gift, each day is a blessing.
So each day passes,
people they will never meet again
are dancing in the sunflower-centre-like clock,
and if there is nothing but this,
this moment's happiness,
then there really is nothing else,
so why am I unable to speak the words

이것 외에 다른 것이 없는데
지금, 이 선물,
왜 나는 이런 말을 못하는가,
트로이에서
허드슨 강변에서
붉은 태양을 품은 푸른 물결 아래
수박의 한가운데 같은 바닥분수의 시간 속에
하얀 편지 같은 갈매기가 날고
물속에서 물고기들 용솟음치고 있는데
강변 공원에 해바라기 복판 같은 여름이 타오르고
몸속에서 쟁 쟁 쟁 커다란 종소리가 울리고
매일매일이 생명의 전성기
이글거리는 노란 화판과 검은 씨 눈동자
이것뿐인데
이것뿐이라면
지금, 이 선물,
더이상은 없다면

푸른 점화

반딧불, 낙서보다 가벼운데,
파르스름하고 희푸스름한 것
떠오르는 순간 투명한 꽁무니에서 빛이 반짝인다
요요하다

(빛이 뜨거우니 아프겠구나)

결국 제 몸에 불을 질러야 반짝일 수 있고
제 몸을 태워 밀고 나가야 떠오를 수 있으니
반디가 떠오르는 것만큼 지평선의 무게는 가벼워지고
파란 점화는 반짝반짝
얼굴의 무게를 뜯어서 들고 간다

now, this gift?
In Troy
beside the Hudson River,
beneath blue waves that embrace the red sun,
in the time of ground-fountains like the heart of watermelons
white gulls like letters wheel
while in the water fish go spurting
and in the park along the river sunflower-centre-like summer blazes,
inside the body the boom, boom, boom of a great bell tolling resounds
day after day, life's heyday,
dazzling yellow petals and black seeds like eyes,
that alone is,
and if that alone is,
now, this gift,
if there is nothing more. . . .

BLUE IGNITION

Firefly, lighter than a scrawl,
something blue and fleetingly white,
as it rises into the air light flashes from its transparent tail.
So remote.

(Light is hot, it must hurt!)

After all, it has to set fire to its body in order to shine
in order to rise it must drive its burning body forward,
so that the weight of the horizon grows lighter, the more the firefly rises,
as the blue ignition sparkles and twinkles,
it removes its face and carries it on its way.

고유의 호흡
고유의 박차
혼자 타는 것들이 빛을 낸다,
혼자 가야 환하다
혼자 가야 환하게 거룩하다

반딧불 날아가는 곳에
어두움밖에 아무것도 없는데
박차고 날아가는 그곳에
어쩐지 영원이 있는 양하다

꽃피는 아몬드 나무

오하이오 주 작은 농촌 마을에서
언니는 아일랜드에 살고 동생은 뉴질랜드에 산다는 여자를
알게 되었다,
야채와 과일 등 유기농 농장을 하는 여자는
토요일이면 파머스 마켓에서 야채, 과일을 팔았다,
여자의 피부는 아몬드 빛, 야채는 늘 싱싱했다,
나도 아들은 토론토에 살고 딸은 뉴욕 주에 살고
나는 서울에 산다고 말했다,
러브 트라이앵글....
여자는 웃었다 먼 거리를 슬퍼하지 않는다
얼굴 한번 보기 어려워도
거기가 멀어질수록 러브 트라이앵글이 커진다고 했다,
물과 달은 어느 대륙이든 다 하나로 통하지요
만해 스님의 「사랑의 측량」?
존 던의 「애도를 금함」에 나오는?
지혜는 밭에서 나온다
여자는 남편은 땅속에 묻혔고
부모님은 하늘의 별이 되었으니
러브 트라이앵글이 더 커졌다고 한다

Special breath,
Special spur,
things that burn alone emit light.
To be bright I must advance alone.
To be brightly sacred I must advance alone.

In the place toward which the firefly is flying
there is nothing but darkness.
In the place toward which it is flying at great speed,
somehow, eternity seems to be there.

AN ALMOND TREE IN BLOOM

In a small rural town in Ohio,
I got to know a woman who told me:
My older sister lives in Ireland and my younger sister lives in New Zealand.
The woman, who ran an organic farm producing vegetables and fruit,
sold vegetables and fruit on Saturdays at the Farmers' Market.
Her skin was almond-coloured, her vegetables were always fresh.
I told her that my son lives in Toronto and my daughter in New York,
while I live in Seoul.
A love triangle. . . .
The woman laughed, saying that distance was not something to be sad about.
Even if it's hard to see their faces,
the greater the distance, the greater the love triangle, she said.
The water and the moon are one in every continent.
As in Ven. Manhae's 'The Measure of Love'?
or in John Donne's 'Forbidding Mourning'?
Wisdom is produced in fields.
The woman had buried her husband in the ground,
her parents had become stars in the sky,
and as a result the love triangle had grown bigger.

바닷빛은 어느 날은 옥색이고 어느 날은 회색이니
사랑의 빛깔은 모른다고 하였다
노란 금작화들이 흐드러지게 타고 있었다
사랑의 풍선이 터지는 것을 많이 본
아몬드 빛 눈이었다

내 속에 내가 마트료시카

내 속에 내가 내 속에 내가 내 속에 내가
두 팔을 흔들며 두 다리를 바둥거리며 두 발을 차며
내 속에 내가 내 속에 내가 내 속에 내가
5피스짜리 마트료시카
내 속에 내가 내 속에 내가 내 속에 내가
바둥거리며 두 다리를 흔들며 두 발을 차며
볼링 핀처럼 우르르 쏟아지며
내 속에 내가 내 속에 내가 내 속에 내가
새벽에
고요한 시간에
내 속에 내가 내 속에 내가 내 속에 내가 내 속에
수원지가 터진 듯 울고 있는
손톱만한 나
궁극의 초상이
5피스짜리 마트료시카 속에 속에 속에 속에
발버둥치며
울며
고요히 도장 뚜껑처럼 딱 몸을 닫는
겨자씨만한
나

She said the sea is the colour of jade one day and grey the next,
so she did not know what colour love might be.
The yellow broom bushes were blooming gloriously.
She had almond-hued eyes
that had seen a host of love balloons bursting.

INSIDE, I'M A MATRYOSHKA DOLL

Waving two arms, flapping two legs, kicking two feet,
the I inside me the I inside me the I inside me,
a 5-fold Matryoshka doll,
the I inside me the I inside me the I inside me,
squirming, flapping two legs, kicking two feet,
the I inside me the I inside me the I inside me,
pouring out like bowling pins,
the I inside me the I inside me the I inside me,
in the quiet time
at dawn,
the I inside me the I inside me the I inside me, inside me
the I the size of a fingernail
crying like a river's source bursting out,
the final portrait,
inside inside inside inside the 5-fold Matryoshka doll,
squirming,
crying,
quietly closing like the cap of a seal,
the size of a mustard seed,
I

멍게

붉은 갑옷을 두르고 싱싱하게 몸부림치면서
푸른 바다에서 헤엄쳐왔건만
너는 도마 위에서 끝난다,
선홍빛 갑옷을 벗기우고
칼 앞에 부드러운 속살이 뭉클거린다,
웃음, 그렇다, 설핏 웃음기 같은 것이 흘렀다,
속없이 어설픈 웃음이 있었다,
푸른 바다를 건너온
수줍은 듯 쓰디쓴 듯 보들보들 보드라운 노란 웃음
모든 웃음은 이빨 달린 웃음이라는데도
멍게 속살은 더할 나위 없이 보드랍기만 하다,
젓가락으로 멍게를 집어 올릴 때마다
그것이 쉽지 않았다는 건
미끄러지는 쾌에 슬픔을 담은 까닭은 아니었을까,
멍게가 설핏 웃는다,
접시 위에 노란 속살을 가지런히 진열하고
이제 더 잃을 것은 없는데
다 끝나서 속이 시원하다는 듯이
속없는 멍게가 노랗게 웃는다

아무도 아무것도

죽음의 문제는 죽음 혼자 풀 수 없고
삶의 문제도 삶 혼자서 풀 수가 없듯이
낮의 문제도 낮 혼자 풀 수 없고
밤의 문제도 밤 혼자 풀 수가 없다

밤의 문제를 밤 혼자 풀 수가 없어
새벽이 오고 태양이 뜨고 대낮이 오듯이
하늘은 바다를 그리워하고
모래도 모래를 그리워할까

SEA SQUIRT

Covered in red armour, squirming fresh
you swam about in the blue sea
but ended up on the chopping board.
Your coral-hued armour is stripped off,
your soft inner flesh quails briefly before the knife.
Laughter, yes, what seemed like laughter emerged,
there was unrestrained, awkward laughter.
Seemingly shy, seemingly bitter, tender, soft yellow laughter
that has swum across the blue sea.
Even though people say that all laughter has teeth,
the inner flesh of a sea squirt is incomparably soft.
Whenever I pick up a sea squirt with my chopsticks
I tell myself that was not easy,
perhaps because there was sorrow in the slippery pleasure.
The sea squirt laughs lightly.
Its yellow flesh once displayed in even strips on a dish,
it has nothing more to lose,
and the voided sea squirt laughs yellow,
as if it feels cool now everything is over.

NOBODY AND NOTHING

Just as the problem of death cannot be solved by death alone
and the problem of life cannot be solved by life alone,
the problem of day cannot be solved by day alone
and the problem of night cannot be solved by night alone.

The problem of night cannot be solved by night alone,
so just as dawn comes, the sun rises, day dawns,
might sky long for sea,
and sand long for sand?

남의 문제를 남 혼자서 풀 수가 없고
북의 문제도 북 혼자서 풀 수 없듯이
나의 문제도 나 혼자 풀 수가 없어
나의 곁에 더불어 네가 있다,
잊어도 좋은데 한사코 너의 이름을, 너의 이름만 부른다

추수감사절 저녁
속을 파내고 불을 켜놓은 커다란 호박의 내부 속에
내부의 사랑을 내부 혼자 풀 수가 없어
코를 파묻고 불 주위를 맴도는 가을 꿀벌처럼
아무도 아무것도 혼자 어둠을 밝힐 수는 없다

막막한 시간

천 번의 천둥이 울어도
천 번의 번개가 잇따라도
비 한 방울 내리지 않는
밤부터 새벽까지 나는 천둥의 숫자를 세어보고 있었다
빗방울의 숫자도 세어보려고 했지만

선거 때만 되면
안 삶은 행주 같은 사람들이 새 옷을 입고
거리 곳곳에 나와 새 행주가 되겠다고
꼭 삶은 행주가, 항균 행주가 되겠다고 난리 아우성치는
우습지도 않은 길목에서

오늘은 오늘의 비가 내리고
내일은 내일의 비가 내렸으면,
(곰팡이는 곰팡이를 반성하지 않고)
오늘의 행주는 꼭 오늘 삶고
잊지 말고, 오늘의 약은 꼭 오늘 먹자

Just as the problems of the South cannot be solved by the South alone
and the North cannot solve the North's problems alone,
I cannot solve my problems alone,
so you are there beside me.
It does not matter if I can forget, still I'm calling your name, your name alone.

Inside a large pumpkin that's been hollowed out, a light lit,
on the evening of Thanksgiving Day,
the inside cannot solve the inside's love alone
but like an autumn bee that buries its nose and goes flying round the light,
nobody and nothing can lighten the darkness alone.

BOUNDLESS TIME

Although thunder pealed a thousand times
and lightning flashed a thousand times,
still not one drop of rain fell
as I counted the thunderclaps from night till dawn.
I intended to count the number of raindrops too, but

When elections come round
people like unboiled dishcloths put on new clothes,
go out, fill the streets and noisily shout that they will become new dishcloths,
newly boiled dishcloths, antibacterial dishcloths,
on street corners that are no laughing matter.

If only today today's rain falls
and tomorrow tomorrow's rain falls,
(mildew does not reflect mildew)
then let's boil today's dishcloth today,
don't forget, and take today's medicine today.

애도 시계

애도의 시계는 시계 방향으로 돌지 않는다
시계 방향으로 돌다가
시계 반대 방향으로 돌다가 자기 맘대로 돌아간다
애도의 시계에 시간은 없다

콩가루도 기도를 할까
콩가루가 기도를 할 수 있을까
콩가루가 기도를 한다면
어떤 기도를 할까
콩가루는 자기를 복원해달라고 기도를 할까
콩가루가 복원될 수 있을까
콩가루에게 어떤 기도가 가능할까

애도의 시계는 그런 기도를 한다
가루가루 빻아져 콩가루들은 날아갔는데
콩가루는 콩가루의 소식을 모르고
콩가루는 콩가루의 주소를 모르고
콩가루는 향수를 모르고

콩가루는 다만 바람 속의 근심으로 바람의 애도를 한다
회오리를 타고 시시때때
애도의 시계는 꿈에서 거꾸로 나온다

저녁의 잔치

저녁, 아직 다 다리가 끊어지지 않은 시간에
야전병원 같은 하루가 진다,
언제 끊어질지 모르는 다리 위에서
노을은 울부짖노라, 왔다갔다하는 하루의 상처가 말도 못하고
쏟아지는 양동이의 피처럼 저물어갈 때
부상병의 하루를 정리하고
기약이 없는 병든 팽이처럼 또 일어나야겠다고

MOURNING'S CLOCK

Mourning's clock does not turn clockwise.
After turning clockwise,
then turning anticlockwise, it turns as it likes.
Mourning's clock has no time

Does bean flour also pray?
Might bean flour be able to pray?
If bean flour prays,
what kind of prayers might it offer?
Might it pray for its own restoration?
Could bean flour ever be restored?
What prayer might bean flour be capable of?

That's the kind of prayer mourning's clock offers.
Once ground to finest dust, bean flour went flying off,
but bean flour knows no news of bean flour,
bean flour does not know bean flour's address,
bean flour knows no nostalgia

Bean flour simply wind-mourns with the anxiety in the wind.
Borne on a whirlwind, sometimes
mourning's clock emerges from a dream upside down.

EVENING'S PARTY

Evening, so long as the bridge has not yet been cut,
spends each day as if it were a field hospital.
On a bridge uncertain when it will be cut,
twilight laments, while the wounds of day come and go, unable to speak
and when the sun sets like blood poured from a bucket
it clears up the day's wounded,
saying they will have to stand up again like sick tops with no appointment.

일어날 수 있겠는가, 뼈의 유령인 팽이여,
다리의 모서리에 걸쳐져서,
정말 광장 앞에는 나동그라진 뼈의 유령들이 즐비하다
부상당한 팽이에게는 역사가 없다,
역사도 상처도 기억도 노여움도 4월 5월도 없이
팽이는 그저 오늘의 채찍으로 오늘 돌고 있을 뿐인데
그런 간신히 팽이를 김수영은 성자라고
바보라고, 야전병원의 하얀 거즈 같은 위로라고도
마지막 힘을 다하여 젖 먹던 힘까지 다하여 팽이는 돌고 있다
바라춤같이 속으로 울며 돌고 있다

내일의 팽이는 어제의 팽이로 급하게 넘어갈까,
아니면 일어나서 한번 더 핑그르르 돌아볼까,
배 넘어가는 순간에 저 혼자 배를 탈출한 선장 같은
대낮에 팬티만 입은 고급 남녀들이 곳곳에서 키를 잡고
중대한 도장을 무섭지도 않게 찍고 있는데, 모두 돌다가 쓰러질까,
이냥 이대로,
노을이 비스듬히 걸린 붉은 다리 끝에 팽이가 돈다

세상의 모든 팽이가 다 쓰러지고 말면
세금은 누가 낼까, 전선은 누가 막을까, 국가는 누가
지킬까, 병원은 누가 간호할까,
(병원이 나를 간호해야지)
(병원을 내가 간호하는) 이 말도 안 되는, 터무니없는,
아픈 팽이에게 세상은 거대 정신병원의 격실과 다름없는,
뇌수를 미싱 바늘로 쪼는 석양의 낭떠러지

사랑할 수 있는 한, 햇빛 한줄기가 있는 한
저녁의 다리가 다 끊어지지 않는 한
영원히 자신을 고쳐가며 일어서고 또 일어서야 할 시간에
아픈 팽이에겐 누더기 같은 역사도 분노도 기억도 없다
쓰러지고 고쳐가고 쓰러지며 또 고쳐가면서
어제와 오늘과 내일이라는 단순을 폐기하며, 단지
평범한 사람의 빛나는 순간을
성자가 될 때까지, 피를 묻히고, 저녁노을 아래서 온몸으로 돌고 돌면서

Will you really be able to stand up again, you top, bone's ghost?
Dangling over the edge of the bridge,
in front of the plaza, the ghosts of fallen bones stand in rows.
The wounded top has no history.
Without history, wounds, memory, anger, April or May,
the top is just being spun today by today's whip.
Such a mere top, the poet Kim Soo-Young once called it a saint,
a fool, a comfort like the white gauze in a field hospital,
while the top spins on, employing its last reserves of strength, the very last,
spins as if dancing a monk's cymbal dance, inwardly weeping.

Will tomorrow's top go rushing over yesterday's?
Or will it just stand up again and go on spinning once again?
Here and there, high-ranking men and women wearing only their underwear
in broad daylight like the captain escaping alone from his sinking ship,
are taking the helm and fearlessly printing grave seals, will they all spin
                                                                              then topple?
Come what may,
the top spins on at the end of the red bridge where dusk hangs aslant.

If all the tops in the world finally topple,
who will pay taxes, who will stop the advancing battle-front, who will guard
the nation? Who will care for the hospital?
(The hospital should care for me)
(but I care for the hospital) absurd, ridiculous,
to a sick top, the world is like a cell in a gigantic mental hospital,
the cliffs of sunset pecking at the brain with a sewing-machine needle.

So long as it can love, so long as there is a ray of sunlight,
so long as the evening's bridge is not cut,
at the time when it has to heal itself and stand up then stand up again, forever,
the sick top has no tatty history, no rage, no memory.
Toppling then healing, toppling then healing again,
discarding the simplicity known as yesterday, today and tomorrow,
until the shining moments of ordinary people
turn into a saint, bloodstained, spinning, spinning on in the twilight glow,

못 박힌 발로 훠이훠이 춤추며
속으로 울며 눈을 감고
일어서는 자의, 비틀거리는 자의, 취한 팽이들의 고요한 춤만
저녁 광장에 조명을 켠 광화문처럼 가득하다

가족사진

어느 가정에나
대개 벽에는 가족사진이 든 액자가 걸려 있다,
부모의 결혼식에서 시작하여 아들딸의 돌 사진,
사각모를 쓴 졸업식, 자식의 결혼식이거나
부모님의 수연(壽宴) 잔치 사진 속에 가족들은 대개 웃고 있다
꽃다발을 사서 들고 생애의 가장 좋은 옷을 챙겨 입었다

액자 속에는
"순간아 멈추어라, 너는 정말 아름답구나"와 같은 슬픔이 깃들어 있다
그 말을 하면 바로 그때 악마가
파우스트의 영혼을 잡아간다는 책이 있었다,
가족사진 속의 웃는 얼굴들이 어딘지 서글픈 것은
그런 말의 포로처럼 순간이 아슬아슬 걸려 있기 때문일 게다

"멈춰라, 순간이여, 너는 진정 아름답구나"
라고 외친 순간에 누군가 영혼을 잡으러 온다고
쓸쓸히 그늘져 보이는 얼굴에
순간 환한 마그네슘 불꽃이 터지고
시간은 화려한 피처럼 거기에서 명멸하듯 멈추었다

dancing wildly with nail-pierced feet,
weeping inwardly, eyes closed,
the quiet dance of the standing-up, tottering, drunken top
fills an evening plaza like Gwanghwamun with the lights on.

FAMILY PHOTOS

In any home
frames holding family photos usually hang on the walls,
starting with the parents' wedding, their children's first birthday,
graduation ceremonies in mortarboards, the children's weddings,
the elderly parents' birthday party, and in such photos the whole family
is usually smiling, holding bouquets, wearing the best clothes of their lives.

In the frames
nestles a sorrow like "Time, stop there, you are so beautiful",
for if he says that, the book tells us,
that's when the devil will seize hold of Faust's soul.
The smiles on faces in family photos are sad
because time is caught there dangerously, as if it's a prisoner of those words.

"Time, stop there, you are so beautiful."
On faces that look forlorn and shaded because they think
someone will come to seize their soul, the moment they exclaim those words,
a momentary magnesium flash has gone off
and time has stopped like bright blood flashing there.

거대한 팽이

너무도 절망이 태연할 때
천지 사방 흩어지는 콩가루 집안처럼 마음이 흩어져서가 아니라
가령 혼자 속으로 울며 무념무사 빙빙 도는 팽이처럼
너무도 절망이 태연하고 깊은 철학이 서린 듯 아름답기까지 할 때
그런 것을 처절한 황홀이라고 하나,
나동그라지다가 일어나 활짝 펼쳐지는 온몸의 파라솔,
고통의 제자리걸음이라기보다
몸에서 몸을 일으키는,
고통이 고통을 넘어 고요 속에 고요의 춤이 가득할 때
(아무도 도와줄 수 없는 팽이의 운명에)
의젓한 중력을 딛고
온몸에 칠해진 팽이의 알록달록 다채로운 색깔이
빙빙 어우러져 급기야 하얀 무지개처럼 솟아날 때
희망에는 증거가 필요하다고 했던 슬픈 거짓말
(쳐라 쳐라 몹시 쳐라, 얼마나 많은 채찍을 넘어왔나)

해는 지고
달은 뜨고
살점을 도려내고 쇠못을 박아
핑그르르 도는 발에서 깊은 피가 흘렀어도
팽이는 너무도 태연한 절망의 팽이 놀리듯
몸에서 몸을 일으키며
제 눈앞의 팽이의 춤을 조용히 건너다보고 있는데
간혹 크낙새 깃 치는 소리만 아득하고
하얀 무지개 춤이 팽이의 배 한가운데서 솟아나는
성스러운 저녁 마당에
(광화문이여, 광화문이여)
누가 팽이와 팽이의 춤을 구별할 수 있는가

팽이가 돌고 있다
천지인 가득 휘영청 팽이들이 돌고 있다
도토리나 상수리, 청설모까지 나와 제 몸을 환히 밝히며 팽이들이 돌고 있다

A HUGE TOP

When despair is excessively calm,
it is not because the heart has scattered in all directions like a broken family.
but when it is quite beautiful
like a top spinning on vacantly, inwardly crying alone,
as if despair were calm and deep philosophy hovering.
Such things are termed gruesome ecstasy
but the body's parasol falling, rising again, opening with a snap,
rather than stationary pain marking time
raising its body up from its body,
when pain goes beyond pain and is full of silence dancing in silence
(in the destiny of a top that nobody can help)
when the variegated colours painted on the top's body
tread on mature gravity
and finally spurt up, blending as it spins into a white rainbow,
the sad lie saying that hope needs evidence
(whip it, whip it hard, just think how many whippings it has already undergone)

The sun sets,
the moon rises,
then after cutting out flesh and driving in iron nails,
even if deep blood comes flowing from the turning feet,
the top seems to be mocking the top of excessively calm despair
as it raises its body up from its body,
quietly looking across at the dance of the top before its eyes
and in a sacred evening garden
occasionally the sound of a woodpecker flapping its wings is faintly heard,
a white rainbow dance emerges from the centre of the top's belly
(Ah, Gwanghwamun. Ah, Gwanghwamun)
Who can distinguish between the top and the top's dance

The top is spinning.
Bright tops are spinning, full of heaven, earth and people.
As acorns, even squirrels emerge, their bodies shining brightly, the tops
                                                                                 are spinning.

나무와 칼과 뼈와 빛으로 빚은 팽이들이
꿈결처럼 조용히 팽이들이 팽이들이 돌고 있다
나도 감히 상상을 못하는 거대한, 거대한 팽이,
누가 꿈과 꿈꾸는 자를, 혁명과 혁명가를 구별할 수 있는가

목에 걸린 뼈

목에 걸린 뼈
3천 마디 몸에 걸린 골절의 뼈
누구의 얼굴을 닮은 것도 같고
누구의 말이 귓가에 남은 것도 같은데
목에 걸린 뼈
어느 약물로도 녹지 않는 뼈
매일매일 슬픈 역사를 적는 일기장 같은 뼈

월요일에 목에 걸린 뼈는
수요일에도 목요일에도 목에 걸려 있고
화요일에 목에 걸린 뼈는 어쩌면 일요일까지도 걸려 있고
다시 월요일로 와서
깊은 밤 광야에서
땅을 붙들고 하늘을 붙들고 울 때
곁에서 통탄하며 울던 뼈

애도 없는 애도의 하늘
광야에서
월요일에도 화요일에도 목요일에도 금요일에도 토요일에도
목에 걸린 뼈, 뼈들이
바람 소리에 피리 소리를 내며 덜그덕거리고 있는데
인간의 악기는 결국 자기 뼈 흔들리는 소리를 내며
운다

Tops made of trees, of swords, of bones, and light,
the tops are quietly spinning like dreams.
A huge, huge top, one I cannot even begin to imagine,
who can distinguish between dream and dreamer, revolution and revolutionary?

A BONE CAUGHT IN THE THROAT

A bone caught in the throat
a fractured bone, 3,000 joints caught in the body,
looking like someone's face,
looking like someone's words lingering in my ears,
a bone caught in the throat,
a bone that no medication will melt,
a bone like the diary where I write sad history day by day.

The bone caught in the throat on Monday
is still caught there on Wednesday and Thursday,
the bone caught in the throat on Tuesday is sure to stay caught until Sunday.
Returning to Monday,
the bone that lamented and wept beside me
as I clung to the ground, clung to the sky and wept
late at night in the wilderness

The sky of mourning devoid of mourning
in the wilderness,
the bone caught in the throat
on Monday, on Tuesday, on Thursday, on Friday, on Saturday,
all those bones
pipe as they rattle when the wind brushes past,
so ultimately the human instrument emits the sound of its bones being shaken
as it weeps.

BIOGRAPHICAL NOTES

Kim Seung-Hee (b. 1952) is now an Emeritus Professor at Sogang University, Seoul, having retired from the Korean Department there in 2017. She has published 10 poetry collections as well as some fiction. She received the 1991 Sowol Poetry Award and the poetry award in Korea's 2006 This Year's Art Awards.

Brother Anthony of Taizé was born in 1942 in England. He completed his studies in Medieval & Modern Languages at Queen's College in the University of Oxford, and holds M.A and M.Litt. degrees. He became a member of the Community of Taizé (France) in 1969. Since 1980, he has been living in Korea. He taught English Literature at Sogang University, Seoul for over twenty years. He is now an Emeritus Professor in the English Department of Sogang University. Since 2010 he has also been a Chair-Professor in the International Creative Writing Center at Dankook University, Seoul.

He has published some 50 volumes of English translations of modern Korean literature, including the novels *The Poet* and *Son of Man* by Yi Mun-Yol and poetic works by Ko Un, So Chong-Ju, Ku Sang, Lee Si-Young, Kim Seung-Hee, Kim Sa-In and others. He was awarded the Korean Government's Order of Cultural Merit (Jade Crown) in 2008. He took Korean citizenship in 1994 and An Seon-jae is his legal Korean name. Since the start of 2011 he has been President of the Royal Asiatic Society Korea Branch. In December 2015 he was awarded an honorary MBE by Queen Elizabeth.

John Kinsella is a poet, novelist, critic, essayist and editor, and has published over thirty books, many of which have won significant literary awards. He is a Fellow of Churchill College, Cambridge University, and Professor of Literature and Environment at Curtin University, West Australia. He is an anarchist vegan pacifist of over thirty-five years and believes poetry is one of the most effecive activist modes of expression and resistance we have.

www.ingramcontent.com/pod-product-compliance
Lightning Source LLC
Chambersburg PA
CBHW031300110426
42743CB00041B/826